My Journal

MW00365769

What do *It's Always Sunny in Philadelphia*, Chipper Jones and WAR, *The Princess Bride*, Hurling, an English explorer in Florida in the 1590s, psychology, Game Theory, the Battle of Waterloo, and a few dozen other equally seemingly unrelated subjects have to do with Family Law?

A lot according to Jenny Bradley's startlingly original take on the law, education, mediation, adultery, and, of course, other lawyers. Inside Baseball from Jenny Bradley, a Family Law Attorney in Cary, North Carolina.

Jenny's a jock, a nerd, and a lawyer. None of that is mutually exclusive. She has been involved in competitions great and small — softball, math bowl, 80's trivia, and bicycling. She loves games. And she loves practicing law. Mostly.

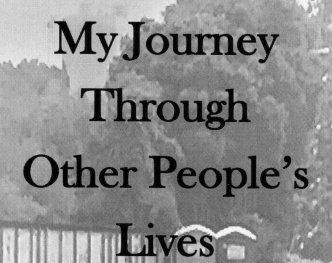

My Journey
Through
Other People's
Lives

By

Jenny Bradley

For more information on the author please go to:

TriangleSmartDivorce.com

<u>*Look for TriangleSmartDivorce on Facebook*</u>

Some of these stories are about me, they are reasonably accurate. Some are client/court studies and while real, have been altered in ways to preserve anonymity and/or confidentiality. Sometimes, I've resorted to Hollywood's well tested condensed characters to make things a bit easier to understand – and for me to write.

One more thing – nothing in this book is legal advice. I'm not your lawyer, you're not my client. If you think you see your particular legal issue somewhere in these pages you are flat out wrong. Law doesn't work that way. Especially family law. If you see your legal issue in these pages run to an attorney.

Tell them my book sent you.

FORLORN HOPE PUBLISHING

To all our clients who have opened their lives to us for protection from others, themselves, and/or the system.
Through you, we have personally and professionally grown deeply and continue to grow each day.
Thank you.

The human ability to rationalize, defend,

and accept our self-imposed drama is bananas.

~ Jen Sincero

Preface

I'm a family law attorney. This was by no means a preordained career.

I, daily, dive into other people's lives. I hear . . . well, everything. Every time I think I've heard it all, I hear something new. People and relationships and families are like that.

I am, then, never bored. Usually this is a good thing. Sometimes it's not. The good outweighs the bad by a wide margin.

Let's get this out of the way right now – I'm a jock, a nerd, and a lawyer. None of that is mutually exclusive.

I have been involved in competitions great and small for most of my life. Softball, math bowl, 80's trivia, and bicycling (in a way). I like competition. I love games. I get my fill of them . . . on my time. Like everyone who plays any game, I like to win. Like anyone who plays any game, I don't like losing.

Competition is great, in the proper venue. Family Law is emphatically not the proper venue. Family law is about resolving, fixing, healing, being reasonable, and moving on.

I've dedicated my practice to helping people move on – I work with clients in family law matters that include premarital agreements, domestic partnership agreements, separation and property settlement agreements, qualified domestic relations orders, and litigation involving property division, alimony, child support and child custody.

I am an active listener and a problem-solver. I understand the financial and emotional vulnerabilities of my clients and use my experience with mediation to resolve many disputes without going inside a courtroom.

My goal in any family law dispute is to make it as worry-free as I can for my client. We will work together as a team to move toward the best resolution possible for your situation, and we will do this as quickly, efficiently and as economically as we can, with your help.

I am the step-mother to a teenager. I personally know the struggles of blended families and how challenging on-going custody and financial issues can be.

I guess what I'm saying is I've lived through many of the things I'm about to write about. I've thought about what my clients go through, what traits great relationships share, what not-so-great relationships have in common, and, well, how we all manage to live and communicate and survive each and every day.

There are some stories about cases I've handled in the upcoming pages – they stand as a microcosm of the many, many cases I've handled and continue to handle every single work day.

Everything else, my thoughts about human nature and all that, are evolving. The one great thing about my career is that I learn something every day.

Jenny Bradley
Cary, NC
December 2018

1. Mail Order

The place to start is with the case that made me think – seriously – about walking away. Not just from family law but from *the* law. Pack it up, toss the casebooks and procedure manuals, and do something – anything – else.

This is where every lawyer reading that paragraph says 'yup, been there' while everyone else wonders when attorneys acquired feelings.

Here's how it went.

Budd was quite simply a good old boy in all the senses of the term. A bear of a guy, the kind you'd have a few Buds with on a rainy Saturday afternoon to comfortably watch any sporting event from baseball to the Olympics to NASCAR, have a solid time, realize when you get home that the two of you may have spoken a combined dozen words all day.

A nice guy. Unfortunately, the exact kind of nice guy Leo Durocher was referencing when he said, "Nice guys finish last."

You would probably not be surprised to learn that Budd was a lonely guy. Hard working, solid guy who desperately wanted female company of a permanent nature, with attendant family.

He married a Japanese mail-order bride. Early on, apparently – it's a little hard to reconstruct now – they got along fine. Budd was … happy. More so after they had two children.

Remember Ferris Bueller? There's a line late in the movie where Ferris looks into the camera and says this about his best friend, Cameron, "He's gonna marry the first girl he lays, and she's gonna treat him like shit, because she will have given him what he has built up in his mind as the end-all, be-all of human existence. She won't respect him, 'cause you can't respect somebody who kisses your ass. It just doesn't work."

Budd was that guy. His wife didn't so much walk all over him as stomp on him. Hard.

He went along with it. All of it. Cooking, cleaning, paying every bill, doting, doing everything for the kids while Ishii watched soaps and hung out.

So, when Ishii started locking her and the kids in a room when he was home, Budd took it in stride, adapted, and began to deliver meals to the door. Later, he'd go back and collect the dirty dishes, wash them, start all over again.

Budd communicated with Ishii via notes he'd leave in the food trays.

I'm sure it bothered Budd, but he was never going to complain to anyone about the situation, as a matter of fact,

I think he was constitutionally unable to complain about anything.

There's no telling, then, how long this would have gone on, but it did stop – Ishii upped the ante one day.

Budd left a meal and a rather bland note for her one morning and headed for work. Ishii took the note and added a death threat from Budd to her on the bottom of the page, what we had was:

> I.
>
> *Hey, hope you guys like the French toast, headed out to work, thinking about spaghetti for dinner, Have a good day. B.*
>
> *FYI, I am going to kill you as soon as I can.*

Ishii called the police, handed the note over, pressed charges while pointing to the fact that she locked herself and the kids in a room whenever her husband was around. We assume she left out all the stuff about his catering meals, though the first part of the note – the part in his handwriting – pretty much belied her point.

Budd was arrested, charged with threatening, child protective services were notified, they immediately launched an investigation.

It was somewhere around here that I became involved, representing Budd as the child protection investigation got underway.

The criminal matter was dropped. The police said they thought Ishii was lying, had forged the note. The prosecutor agreed, the charges were dropped. This, though, did not stop the child protection investigation from continuing.

Budd popped home just long enough for Ishii to claim domestic violence. Another criminal investigation was launched.

With the previous arrest, despite being dismissed, on top of the pending domestic abuse allegation, the court considering the child protection case couldn't afford to be anything but cautious. The judge ordered that Budd could only have supervised visits with his children for the time being.

The plan was that when the domestic abuse investigation was completed and no charges were levied, Budd would upgrade to unsupervised visits. Which was all that Budd wanted. In life.

The domestic abuse case was dropped.

Ishii refused to comply with the court order, refused to let Budd visit with his children.

We filed a contempt motion in court for Ishii's failure to comply with the judge's order. We went to court, Budd and I sat together and watched Ishii's lawyer fire her:

"You lied," the lawyer said, "I'm out of here, I'm withdrawing. Now." Mic drop and out of there.

Without a lawyer, Ishii asked for a continuance. To hire a new lawyer with Budd's dwindling supply of money and regroup.

The judge really had no choice but to grant it, ruling against Ishii when she didn't have a lawyer was only going to result in Ishii showing up with one and starting all over again.

So, no decision. Ishii has her continuance and goes home with the kids while Budd's stuck in law purgatory.

A few days later, Budd drives by the house, probably in the hope of glimpsing the kids for a few minutes. First thing he notices is that the outside water is on and his lawn is a small but growing lake.

He pops out of the car to turn the water off, looks in a window to find that the house was completely, totally empty.

Ishii took off with the kids and every one of the marital possessions doing to Budd what the Baltimore Colts did to Baltimore when they slunk out of town in the dead of night for Indianapolis.

There were two mysteries: no one saw a moving van, so how'd she get everything out? Where did she and the kids go?

The latter took a bit of research, before we confirmed that Ishii had fled to Japan. A little more digging and we found out that, unbeknownst to Budd, she got the kids Japanese passports.

Once we figured that out, we discovered, after Budd looked at his credit card and bank statements, that Ishii had quite simply shipped all their stuff to Japan piece by piece. Like the guy in *MASH* who mailed a jeep home to Idaho.

Let me take the suspense out of the rest of this story – we couldn't touch them in Japan. Japan was not a signatory to the Hague Convention and does not honor or enforce court orders from the United States.

We got the U.S. State Department involved. Through their Japanese Embassy they found Ishii and the kids at her mother's house. The kids were fine.

That was all the help they could offer. Someone from the Embassy could look in on the kids – they were, after all, at least for the time being, still American citizens. But that was and is the extent of it.

Along with this – if Budd flew to Japan to see the kids and Ishii objected and called the police … well, he'd be in a really bad spot.

At this point you may be wondering why this case? Why is this the one that hit me so hard? After all, there are worse sets of facts in some of the other stories in this book.

Because this: talking with Budd while trying to see if there was a Hail Mary we could toss, here or in Japan before we accepted fate, Budd told me that after Ishii started to lock him out of rooms, he pulled his sponsorship of her visa. Which then expired.

Ishii could have been deported if she did not voluntarily leave the U.S. She'd have to leave the kids, U.S. citizens that they were, in joint custody of Budd.

There is, however, an exception — for women who claim abuse. They are automatically stayed from any State Department action (or most certainly were in 2008, when this all happened).

Her allegations started the stay. Budd was removed, however temporarily, as a parent with full custody rights. With no contact with them, he was out in right field while Ishii went about arranging Japanese passports.

Ishii had a male friend in Maryland. Phone bills showed they talked and texted a lot. We discovered he was an immigration lawyer.

Suddenly, nothing Ishii said or did looked like it was accidentally so serendipitous for her. Everything she did was obviously completely, utterly perfectly planned.

She wanted to ditch Budd, take the kids and whatever assets she could grab, and move back to her real home.

As it began to sink in, I felt like the detective at the end of *Wild Things,* standing in the parking lot as the brother of the woman she assumes is dead explains, "Old lady had her tested once. They said her I.Q. was way up there... around two hundred or some such . . .She could do just about anything she put her mind to."

Ishii was so far ahead of us she was playing a different game.

Every step of the way, right down to getting the continuance and the time she needed to wrap it all up without interference.

She left the water on at the house just to let Budd know she was gone and he had lost.

We did everything we could do under the laws of North Carolina to do the right thing, get Budd time with his kids, work things out.

Obviously, never Ishii's goals.

From an emotional standpoint, we felt powerless and used, with me wondering for months if there was anything else I could have done, anything I missed.

Bill Murray's attorney character figured it out in *Wild Things,* why didn't I?

2. Aspirations

I have an associate, Lauren, who grew up in a small city in Ohio, the daughter; of the quintessential and once ubiquitous small-town general practitioner attorney.

From cradle to middle school her father would tell her she could be anything she wanted to be, the sky was the limit ... but, please, don't be a lawyer.

That, of course, firmly fixed the thought of being a lawyer firmly in her mind. When it became evident, in her teens, that Lauren was on a laser beam path to law school, her father's plea became, "Okay, just, please, don't be a family law attorney."

That, again of course, solidified Lauren's choice of profession and area of concentration – I hired her as a family law associate in 2017; she came with years of experience.

I'm not like Lauren, I had no thought of growing up to be an attorney; I didn't watch L.A. Law as a kid; I didn't have a lawyer father advising me on career choices in any direction; I didn't grow up in a tidy, progressive small city.

I grew up in a small town on the fringes of the Great Smokey Mountains National Park. Blount County, Tennessee is never going to be immortalized like Faulkner's Yoknapatawpha County. The best it can hope for, with its solid Scots-Irish heritage, is a passing mention in books like *Hillbilly Elegy* and *White Trash: A History The 400-Year Untold Story of Class in America*.

Blount County's too far off the beaten path to be anywhere near the center of those books, hell, even Harlan County, Kentucky – made famous by *Justified* – is 140 miles dead north.

Maybe all I need to explain – and all you need to know – about Blount County and the nearby city of Maryville is that the town of Alcoa is exactly 2.37 miles from the center of Maryville and, for all intents and purposes, the center of the county.

The steel/aluminum company was not named for the town. ALCOA came to Blount County in 1907, stayed, took over as the center of, well, everything.

To say 'as ALCOA goes, so goes the county' was as true in the 1910s as it is today. The results since the late 1960s are obvious and show in every storefront in downtown Maryville. I've often wondered if Blount County is the southernmost Rust Belt community.

About my childhood in that rapidly drying up town: there weren't all that many happy people. At least, not that I, my family, or anyone I knew could attest to.

A lot of family law attorneys, okay, the well-read ones, like to quote Tolstoy and the opening line of *Anna Karenina.*, "Happy families are all alike; every unhappy family is unhappy in its own way."

That did not apply to my childhood. I doubt it applies to anyone of Scots-Irish descent, particularly those who inhabit the same hills, dales, hollers, of the ancestors who flooded in to America and the mountains of North Carolina during the rebellions and civil wars of the late 17th and early 18th Centuries and had only managed to move a few hundred miles west since.

Generations of Scots-Irish who have lived in our hills with the men only venturing out to harass Red Coats, tramp up to Gettysburg, down to Cuba, over to France while ALCOA was annexing a chunk of the county, back to France again, up to Korea . . . and on and on.

The children – the 1980s children – of those men and the women who stayed put, myself very much included, then, would say 'every unhappy family was pissed off for entirely different reasons but as far as the outside world, i.e. everyone not family, was concerned we handled it exactly the same: we internalized and put on a brave face and went on with whatever we needed to move on with.' Acknowledge a problem? In the grave, maybe.

Happy people were different.

My family lived in a single-wide trailer by the cliched but very real railroad tracks. We had plenty of company.

I had a troubled, perhaps very troubled, upbringing – for various reasons. How troubled, looking back from a very safe distance, varies according to when I choose – by accident or design – to think about it. It's a comfort to me that I think about it much less these days than I ever have and I envision the trend continuing.

Parents.

My mother wanted to be a nurse. That hope started to fade when she became pregnant with me when she was sixteen and still in high school. Then, her brother was shot dead on their front steps. Really. She had to raise her younger brother. Then I came along and she got to take care of me as well.

At times, my and my uncle's subsequent appreciation for such an act of selflessness could be measured only by the same instruments CERN uses to detect the Higgs boson.

Mom never did get to nursing school, but she did take several college classes, earned her certificate in medical coding and settled into a career as a medical office administrator.

Dad was exactly *that* steelworker so out of date yet currently in the news every day, bitter and embattled long before Trump discovered his sub-species. He worked for ALCOA – note that the past tense has been applicable for a while.

Aside helping him with anything mechanical, after about age 10 we did not get along – an understatement, but enough for now.

Most of all our relationship felt like we were in a years long competition for some unknown prize until the day I left for college.

Everyone I knew beyond nodding to on the street had some family issue or another ready crisis. We'd see glimpses at times, hear a whisper or two, rarely discuss it openly – and then usually only when they hit the front page of *The Daily Times*.

As happened more than once.

Had we, at any point before high school, sat down to swap family horror stories I have no doubt it would have – within minutes – devolved into the Monty Python sketch with the middle-aged men one upping one another with, "You were lucky to have a bed, we had to …" and on and on.

To recap: Mom a bit psychically bruised and working in a job more than a few steps below her aim and abilities; Dad a last bastion of a dying industry; Scots-Irish; Southern Baptist (it didn't, then or now, take hold with me); low-middle class (or poor as I now know it); as an infant, both parents were in high school; lived with grandparents before the train tracks; in a town centered around said dying industry; surrounded by beautiful mountains usually encased in cloud and fog; eventually moved into a house with a mortgage at 12% interest, thinking we were really making it.

I, though, had two things going for me – I was a good athlete and I not only loved to learn, I wanted to learn stuff on my own.

I learned to read before I went to school. As my mother tells it, one day she looked down and realized I was reading the newspaper. No, I don't know how or why, just that it seemed like the thing to do at the time.

Looking back, it's probably the most fortuitous thing I did in my life. Ever. It shocked my mother. She never forgot it.

She didn't forget it when I started grammar school in our un-consolidated school district – no one was crossing any railroad tracks in any direction to get to school.

It was . . . uninspiring. Almost insipid. Trying to learn anything above the curriculum that probably hadn't been changed since the Johnson Administration was impossible within the four walls of the school.

I was, in fact, discouraged from venturing beyond what was taught. It was either a case of 'why shoot high and be crushed later on,' or 'who are you to think you can be better than everyone else,' I never figured it out.

I know I was frustrated, I can't begin to conjure up today, typing this, behind my desk, in my office smack dab in the middle of The Research Triangle, surrounded by top-flight universities, knowledge at my finger tips and in the air like pollen, what being cut off from 'learning stuff' felt like.

I just know it wasn't good and I didn't do well with it.

It was a struggle that, despite any family dysfunctions, did not go unnoticed. My parents saw I was ahead of my classes, saw that I read things not remotely on the syllabus (had one existed), was constantly exploring subjects I was never going to run into in the school I was in as well as the high school I was headed for.

Somewhere, somehow, they noticed all that. Somewhere, somehow, they decided I deserved a better life. Somewhere, somehow, they came up with the tuition to send me to school in the 'city' – Maryville.

It changed everything.

§

I don't know anyone who would willingly relive their high school years. Kathleen Turner in *Peggy Sue Got Married*, maybe, but who else? It would be just too damn gut wrenching, not to mention repetitious.

I'm no different. High school was as remarkably confusing, embarrassing, and bewildering for me as everyone else. But, there's a but.

High school opened me up to a world I suspected – from a distance – but never verified, out there beyond my neighborhood, the train tracks, the town, the mountains, the state.

I had grown up curious, as I wrote earlier, but in the pre-Internet age, somewhat restricted by the parameters of my Scots-Irish-on-off-Southern-Baptist life.

In other words, the pursuit of knowledge for the sake of knowledge was not exactly a something one did where I grew up.

I heard and read the usual litany of Bible stories, I read the books I had to read in grammar school, they all added up to a very insular worldview . . . if, indeed, I had one at all.

So, again, high school.

I was amazingly lucky. I was lucky my parents recognized my apparently very evident need/wish to learn everything I could possibly learn about anything I could possibly learn about.

I was lucky they decided to support that need, I was lucky the town had an extraordinary school, I was lucky my parents decided to pay tuition to that school despite our circumstances.

I was, then, already lucky when I walked through the doors of the school, so it became, then, a sort of miracle when I ended up with an English teacher with a PhD., a passion for teaching, and the ability to actually do it.

Dr. Penny Ferguson introduced me to the Western Civilization canon and welcomed me to cram every book I could into my head. Every book.

Sports and books may sum up my entire high school experience. Or, books and sports, it's hard to put it in the right order.

There were other great teachers at my high school. I always

She finished what she started

single out Dr. Ferguson, though, because she unlocked something. Or encouraged something. Or recognized something.

Whatever it was, it did this: made me completely open to learning. Whatever I could. In whatever subject I happened to be exposed to at the time.

I was good at it. Learning, that is. And that inspired some confidence. Which, most people would agree, I think, is a very precious commodity for anyone to possess in high school.

So, yeah, sports and books . . .and I graduated with honors. And, along with my grandmother. Really. As the article says, she went back while I was there and 'finished what she started.'

College was bewildering in a different way. I wanted to major in everything. Philosophy, Psychology, Bioethics, economics (especially Third World), softball (I founded the women's softball team . . . someone had to).

I finally settled on psychology, it seemed to encapsulate a lot of other disciplines. Did it foreshadow my becoming a family law attorney?

Not even a little.

I became an RA. An RA with a one set of rules: 'If I don't hear it, see it, smell it, or have it puked on me, it's not there. If I have to wake up to deal with something, someone's getting written up."

As a day to day philosophy of what I expect from other people, it worked well then and has held up pretty well ever since.

The problem with college is they kick you out after four successful years and they don't hand you a life user's guide on the way out.

I, however, wanted to stay in school and, well, learn stuff. So, I decided to go to graduate school. A graduate school. In virtually any discipline. Just someplace that would let me keep going to classes. Preferably not in the snow.

I decided to take the GRE and the LSAT. The Graduate Record Examinations could lead to advanced degrees in anything from Archeology to Zoology and everything in between.

The LSAT was for law school.

I vowed that I'd follow the path of whichever test I scored higher in, despite the rather narrow trail a good score on the LSATs offered.

I nailed the LSAT.

I nailed it well enough to get into the University of North Carolina School of Law.

That's how I became an attorney. I suspect that's how most attorneys become attorneys.

3. Court

So ... before I go back to more cases, I thought I'd do a quick segue to the elephant in every room when it comes to any law related writing: Court.

Mention that you're an attorney, particularly a family law attorney, to anyone and you can expect one of two responses. Either, "Oh, really, hey, let me ask you [intensely personal legal issue goes here]"; or, "Wow, court must be intense! Got any cool stories?"

My advice to new lawyers, by the way – if you're at the proverbial cocktail party and the same person asks both questions . . . suddenly notice an old friend across the room, feign illness, run. What's coming next, you *really* want nothing to do with.

I should state this up front, I'm good in court. I'm comfortable in court. Court is, in my opinion, the last option for most family law matters, the place very – very – few clients should ever want to go. For one simple reason – once you walk into a court room, the outcome is out of your hands. It has shifted to a stranger (or worse, strangers) and an element randomness enters the picture.

Over the last few years I've written a bit about court – not cases – a lot. These are the pieces I think do the best job of conveying my philosophy about taking a case to court.

Sometimes, of course, court cannot be avoided – spouses are too far apart for any hope at an agreement, there are serious issues that absolutely necessitate judicial intervention, to name two.

For all the other cases, however . . . well, just a word to the wise, after all my firm's motto is "We stop smart people from screwing up their divorces."

§

"I want my day in court."

I get this from clients I have just started representing on an almost daily basis. It isn't necessarily stated exactly like that, but the tone and inference is clear – 'the judge will get me, she'll know how wronged I've been ... I'll be vindicated (or similar verb) . . .'. You get the picture.

When they finish, I wait a short moment before I paraphrase *The Princess Bride's* Inigo Montoya: "About going to court – '*I do not think it means what you think it means*'."

Clients, I have found over the years, think court and conjure up clean, quick images from *Law & Order*, or any dozen or so other TV shows where everything is solved in a nice, tidy forty-seven minutes.

TV doesn't show the hours and hours of preparation for trial; depositions, paperwork, interviews, motions, briefs. Hours of work that have to be paid for. It doesn't show the stress of that preparation, the stress of moving through the trial itself, the continuances, delays, surprises, conflicts.

It certainly doesn't show the aftermath, the scars, hard feelings, lasting antipathy.

There aren't any shows about mediation. It's what I do and I'll be the first to admit I'd be bored stiff watching it.

That's the point. Trials are inherently dramatic; mediation is not.

Trials are in your face, conflict ridden, win or lose, propositions. Mediation is working it out.

Trials are about the single-minded quest for validation, or, way too often, revenge.

As to that, Inigo Montoya is even more to the point, "There's not a lot of money in revenge."

§

Going to court requires immense preparation. Every time. Anything less is like the coach blowing off the week before the Super Bowl because he's coached other games.

It is daunting. It is expensive.

There's another element to a court appearance that bears careful consideration – as I explain to clients. Yes, you will get a chance to tell your side of the story. Yes, the judge will listen. Yes, I will ask all the questions we need so that you can get your side of the story out in a comprehensive, coherent manner.

You could be on the stand for hours. The other side will grill you, but I'll help get you through it. Then, we'll parade your witnesses up, one after the other, to really flesh out and back up your story.

What could go wrong?

The answer to that is Harvey Haddix.

What does a decent left-handed starting pitcher from the '50s and '60s have to do with court?

Everything.

On May 26, 1959 Harvey Haddix started for the Pittsburgh Pirates against the defending National League Champion Milwaukee Braves. Harvey threw nine perfect innings. No runs, no hits, no errors. Unfortunately, the score at the end of nine was 0-0.

Harvey pitched a perfect tenth. Then a perfect eleventh. And a perfect twelfth. The Pirates had twelve hits but could never manage to score.

In the bottom of the 12th, Harvey lost the perfect game when he – probably very sensibly – walked Hank Aaron. His next pitch to Joe Adcock was deposited over the right-centerfield wall for a game winning . . . double. Adcock was so excited he sprinted around the bases and passed Aaron, thereby insuring that the final score was 1-0.

Harvey Haddix did what no one had ever done or has done since – he was perfect through twelve innings. Harvey's teammates did, well, nothing. Harvey got the loss.

What of it? Simple – if you insist on going to court understand that you and your witnesses and me have to be perfect. For that one day, five, six hours or more, we all have to be perfect. And there are always – always – factors that are out of our control even if we are perfect.

Everyone involved has to give the performance of a lifetime in court, a Lady Gaga at the Superbowl level performance.

And, like poor Harvey Haddix, you still never know, perfection is not always rewarded.

§

Tom Holland wrote a series of books about the Roman Empire. They are fascinating and highly entertaining. Holland has a wicked sense of humor (and irony) and doesn't spare any of his 'characters' – it really makes for a different history read.

Most people know our system of law descends directly from

the Romans. Holland gives a great description of the way Roman law worked in the first book of his series, *Rubicon*. Actually, he gives several great descriptions as he relays – blow by blow – some of the more famous trials of Roman history before the Republic ended after the rise of Julius Caesar.

Some of it is instantly recognizable to anyone who has ever spent more than a few minutes in a modern-day courtroom. Judge, jury, prosecutor, defense attorney, spectators, arcane rules of procedure rigorously applied.

The Romans had all that, in spades. Drop any one of my colleagues or clients into a Roman court in 25 BC and, outside the fact the trial was probably being held outdoors, they'd be comfortable in the setting, know where to sit and what to do. The Latin might be a problem, but even then more than a few words would make perfect sense.

The juries then were larger – much larger – twenty-four to thirty-six citizens, sometimes more. Spectators could number in the thousands – think civil lawsuits held in the Dean Smith Center.

There were magistrates who specialized in the intricacies of the law, but they rarely presided over trials. The judges tended to be citizens trusted to be impartial, with the temperaments of NBA referees.

Lawyers could be anyone. Well, any male citizen of the Republic. Prosecutors and defense attorneys had day jobs as merchants, farmers, up and coming politicians, senators.

An aggrieved party could ask anyone to act as a prosecutor for them. The accused could ask anyone to defend him. Even then, it was generally accepted that only idiots acted as their own attorneys.

Family matters, by the way, didn't go to court. Divorces in ancient Rome were granted when the husband (and sometimes the wife or her family) said the marriage was over.

"Hi, honey, we're divorced, catch you later," was legally sufficient.

Trials in Rome weren't necessarily only contests between the plaintiff and defendant. They could take on an entirely different importance when the prosecutor and defense attorney had their own political agendas to pursue far beyond whatever the case was about.

Some defense attorneys, men like Cicero, defended cases solely to defeat the prosecutor, usually another politician. Those matters became a contest between lawyers with scarcely a thought given to why they were opposing one another in the first place. Jurors could easily get sucked into the contest of personalities.

Jury decisions were by majority opinion. Bribery was frowned on, but it happened with little to no repercussions beyond public opinion, a wildcard that could never be discounted. Spectators could get wild and their actions could most certainly sway juries concerned about getting home in one piece.

The similarities with our system are obvious, and they are stark.

One thing, though, rings true for both - you take a case to court, anything can happen.

§

I mentioned surprises a few pages ago – as in how incredibly unpleasant it is when a surprise pops up just before or during a trial. Take a surprise and a series of 'tail flip' decisions by the presiding judge and you have my nightmare scenario.

Or, Netflix's big hit *The Staircase*.

Like me, many of you may remember the case, having – in many cases unwillingly, it was that pervasive – seen it covered every day on local TV here in North Carolina.

It was impossible to miss the arrest, trial and the subsequent appeal(s) in 2015, thirteen years after it all started.

On the off chance you didn't live in North Carolina when it went down, or were in a coma, here's a recap:

A writer, Michael Peterson, called 911, said he found his wife, Kathleen, lying at the bottom of a staircase in their mansion in Forest Hills, screamed that she was bleeding profusely.

She died before the ambulance arrived. He told the paramedics and police he found her at the foot of the stairs. The police claimed he bludgeoned her to death.

He was arrested, charged with murder, hired an all-star defense team, went to trial, was convicted, appealed eight years later, won the appeal, was released from prison, cut a deal with the prosecutor, and stayed home for good.

The series is thirteen episodes long so, yes, there's a lot more to it. A French film crew started following everyone involved in the case – on both sides – very early on; the coverage was extensive, award winning, and almost surreal in its depth.

If you binged it on Netflix, or remember it live, you probably have an opinion, perhaps even a strong one, concerning Michael's guilt or lack thereof.

That's great, but not why I'm writing this.

This is about how pieces of *The Staircase* perfectly illustrate many of my feelings about going to court. This was a murder case, so obviously, aside a plea deal, it was always headed for court, that takes nothing away from its instructional value.

Spoilers ahead, maybe.

Surprising your attorney with a nugget of information they really should have known the day you hired them is never a good thing. In fact, surprises are bad after the first consultation; really bad just before depositions; terrible during a deposition; beyond horrific on the eve of trial.

Peterson did it to his legal team ... twice. After a few months of investigation his lawyers were shocked to discover – from a local TV station's evening news – that their client had had a series of one-night stands and casual sexual encounters with men for years that his wife may or may not have known about.

No matter, the existence of any number of emails were motive for the prosecution, another thing to explain for the defense, bad.

On the eve of trial, Peterman's attorneys were watching the same local news station when a special news bulletin informed them that years earlier, when Peterson was living in Germany, he found his next-door neighbor dead ... at the bottom of her staircase.

The German authorities called the death 'natural' but talk about bad optics.

Peterson's failure to disclose this little nugget was devastating – it came out of nowhere just when the defense thought they had everything set for their case.

Think ten minutes before the Super Bowl and Tom Brady tears a hamstring in the tunnel on the way out for introductions.

By the way, at the time Peterson had spent about $350,000 on his defense and now his attorneys had to immediately send their investigator to Germany. That was not cheap. When lawyers are forced to scramble, the meter pretty much runs like it did on the guy in the taxi in *Airplane!*

Another one of my motifs over the years: a lot of uncertainty accompanies every court appearance. An attorney can only control so much.

Judge's decisions, moods, likes, dislikes, and every other thing that makes them as human off the bench as the rest of us are not necessarily 'predictable.'

In the last episode of the series, the filmmakers sat down with the judge. He comes across, as he had throughout the trial and appeal, as a decent guy, smart, sense of humor, who had clearly had his fill of the case over 13 years.

He very candidly said he wasn't sure now – today – he'd make the same rulings against Peterson that he made in the original trial. These were make or break rulings on matters of admissibility that probably swung the case against Peterson.

The judge had been thinking about his decisions for years, questioned them now, rued about how close they were.

Which, of course, is always one of my major concerns– the wild card court variable of humans making decisions in the moment that have earth shattering effects for years.

What do I take out of *The Staircase*? Easy, tell your attorney everything, upfront; surprises in court cases are only fun in novels and movies; resolve as much as you can, when you can, leaving as little as possible to a court hearing and …don't go in the first place if you can reasonably avoid it.

§

I just realized I used a 'Super Bowl' metaphor at least twice in this chapter. I was going to go back and change one of them when this thought hit me : '*Leave it. Going to court over a family matter is your Super Bowl. Like the New York Jets, it's also most likely your only appearance.*'

4. Three Bedsheets

I was – as I do with every 'old' case I write about – trying to think of a short phrase to describe one of the parties.

In this matter two words came to me the second I put pen to paper and those two words – like a bad disco era song – would not get out of my head.

So...

...Batshit crazy.

Rhonda was batshit crazy.

It didn't creep up to me as the case went on. It was evident from the first time we met. In retrospect, I just didn't appreciate the upper levels of a truly batshit crazy woman.

The facts: Rhonda and her husband, Rick – a Dominican here on a green card – were married, separated, married, separated, married, and separated more times than I care to count.

They were, in fact, serial separators.

Once upon one of the separations they signed an agreement that laid out support and a discussion of property.

Or so we thought. Apparently, the very act of negotiating consummated by signing the agreement spurred them into another reconciliation.

It didn't last any longer than any of their other reconciliations and they headed back to court, apparently set on actually divorcing – or maybe they had been in court so often they had made lifelong friends that they missed.

In any event, we ended up going to trial where the issues were whether that agreement was still valid and if so, was it applicable to the property they had acquired *after* they signed the agreement?

Perfectly legitimate you may be murmuring to yourself.

I would agree except for this: the history of separations and reconciliations.

Discovery showed that this wasn't a matter of love, hate, passion, cooling, rediscovered ardor and everything that would make a half decent '90s romcom starring Matthew McConaughey and Sarah Jessica Parker.

They separated or stayed married whenever they had an issue with naturalization, the green card, the IRS, and a host of other legal and financial issues.

One marriage was solely to avoid having the IRS seizing one of Rick's businesses.

The details aren't important, what's important is that the whole married-separated-married gig paid handsomely.

It was inevitable someone somewhere would eventually catch on.

As our judge did.

"You all have claimed whatever marital status that happened to benefit you most at the time. You're – that's both of you – aren't credible...at all.

"You know what? I'm saying you signed an agreement, I didn't rescind it, no one else rescinded it – we're sticking to it.

"Have a great day."

Rhonda started fidgeting at the top of the judge's soliloquy, picked up speed halfway through, hit full throttle towards the end.

She jumped up, began screaming, "It's not true...none of that's true!" She had gone full batshit crazy.

That became her mantra, the judge didn't seem to care, he finished and was probably thrilled to be done with her.

Except she wasn't going anywhere as long as there was an audience.

She was still yelling when I took her by one elbow and my partner took her by the other and we began to steer her out.

She resisted, we picked her up by those elbows and walked her, feet dangling, out of the court room.

Rhonda fired us.

A few weeks later she started spray painting sheets, hanging them all over her property by the roadside.

"NO JUSTICE."
"THE COURT HATES WOMEN."
"THE JUDGE DIDN'T LISTEN."

And more screeds, so I'm told, I never drove by though I did see some local news piece on her laundry protest.

I like to think those sheets, yellowed, torn, paint fading are still there blowing tattered in the breezes, silent testimony to batshit crazy.

§

I'm all for the legalization of marijuana. This is my evidence for it:

Sam and Molly have one kid. Sam and Molly are, by their own admission and various smells that linger on them, their car, and their house, potheads.

They've lived together for some time, but never married, had one child.

They've decided to split, both love the kid, now 8 years old. Molly wants to move to upstate New York, Sam loves North Carolina – his mom and dad are here, the kid's school is here, Sam has a job and, more importantly, plans for the future.

Molly has no job, no plans, just wants to live with her mom and sister.

They're not strident about any of this. They both say what they want, they both can see why the other wants what they want.

They both want custody, they both know they can't have sole custody.

They are relaxed, they are also very much adults.

We worked it out; the kid spends the school year with dad, summers in New York.

No court, no lawyers, just a mediator (me!) and a couple of meetings over two months.

Resolved, everybody is on their 'Merry Way.'

Legalize it and pass it out before every mediation session.

I have a feeling this will go a bit smoother.

§

Sometimes a case – a single case – spirals out of control and everything that can go wrong does and will go wrong. Without exception.

That's Ron's case. Multiple jurisdictions. Dozens of court appearances (I'm being conservative here). Many court orders. Many violated court orders. Contempt motions everywhere.

And worse – far worse – three children swept up in years of court machinations.

Briefly: Ron lived in Rhode Island, was married to Bridget, they had three kids. He went into companies that were in distress and found ways to wind them down without having to resort to bankruptcy. She was a scientist for Big Pharma.

They filed for divorce. It went badly form the rip, Bridget didn't respond well to judicial requirements, never mind the judge's orders, Ron filed numerous contempt motions.

The divorce, contentious for no reason I can ascertain beyond Bridget's 'why make anything easy for this guy' attitude, was granted, Bridget moved – with the kids – to North Carolina, Ron remarried. This time with a prenuptial agreement in place. Ron's a learner.

I came into the matter not long after Bridget moved here because almost simultaneous with the last box being unpacked in her new house, she refused to comply with Rhode Island's visitation order. No visits. Period.

Then she refused to comply with other court orders. Then Ron lost his job, his income plummeted, and he needed to modify his child support.

Bridget may have been a serial court order violator, but she sure as hell wasn't happy Ron needed to modify one. She went Looney Tunes (a family law term of art). She did everything she could – and more – to obstruct every court proceeding. She wielded the children as a weapon while doing so.

Ron eventually decided to not pursue custody of the children, stop filing contempt motions, in general to just stop fighting the lunatic in the hopes that the thing would wind up and the 'kids would come around.'

He got his child support modification. Bridget promptly took a new job in Minnesota and split with the kids. She pretends North Carolina never happened. She did not do this in the abstract, she did it in court by filing for back support from Rhode Island.

Multiple hearings, a special master appointed, appeals, it turned an already far too long, far too complicated, far too stressful case into a Dickens novel.

All the legal machinations above took years, of course. Looking at those paragraphs I realize a summation like this does no justice to the time all this took. Nor does it convey the . . . aura that hung over this for years. This was the case that was always there for Ron. Always.

And while this was pending, the kids were hardly immune to all the issues swirling around their parents. It affected them all. Each child went through their own issues. Each child had to get through those while dealing with the never-ending family drama(s).

It was rough. They came through it. Somehow fittingly, I think, it was their great relationship with their stepmom – dad's new wife that really helped.

They do not enjoy anywhere near as good a relationship with mom. Though they do like her new husband.

§

Speaking of never-ending cases, this one is still hanging out there. Jim is a military aviator. Pam is a grammar school teacher, they have two children.

Jim is not a perfect husband or dad, he's away a lot to boot. Mom is not a perfect wife or mother though she is around a lot. They have issues. They do not talk. Much.

The only two things they agree on is that they are each always right and the other is always wrong.

Okay, this is not all that unusual for a family lawyer like me. Could be close to the norm, actually.

So, this would hardly be a 'noteworthy' case except for this: Pam's way of filing for divorce was to file two domestic violence complaints against Jim.

Enter Jenny.

The domestics were dismissed. Quickly.

Pam immediately filed 3 emergency custody actions.

All denied.

Pam packed up the kids and moved to Florida.

We filed an emergency custody action and brought the kids back to North Carolina. We had a custody hearing and the Judge ruled that if Pam stayed here custody would be evenly split between Jim and Pam. If Pam insisted on staying in Florida, Jim would get primary custody.

Very straightforward, we thought.

Pam packed the kids up and zipped back to Florida.

The rest of this story, as you've probably guessed, is pretty much Christopher Nolan's *Memento* without the cool plot.

Also, that movie was fun for ninety-eight minutes, Jim and Pam are still at it.

§

I offer this without judgment or opinion.

Burns and Margret went to college together, he went on to medical school, they had three children, she stayed home to raise them.

Burns became a doctor and picked up a second career engaging in affairs with various members of his various staffs.

Margret finally caught on and filed.

Burns, probably obviously, was and is a narcissist, but probably not a Class A one – he felt some guilt.

Maybe more than some, because in extraordinarily sort order, he:

> Signed over all the equity in their house.
>
> Agreed to pay the mortgage until the last
> kid was 18.
>
> Agreed to pay 80% of his income to
> Margret as child support.
>
> Ceded custody to Margret and agreed to
> visits when she agreed to them.

Margret ended up a single mom in a free house with a generous stipend backed by life insurance. Burns only shows up for school and sports events.

He comes stag.

§

Computer people.

Gordon was an exec, Donna was a computer engineer. They had two children, one in high school and one in middle school.

They got along just fine. They talked. They shared. They wanted to divorce.

Now.

Gordon hired me. He hired me with this, his sole stipulation: 'get 'er done.'

We went to our first meeting with Donna and her lawyer on their home field — a office with a magnificent lobby complete with a fountain.

On our way to the meeting, Gordon stopped to admire the fountain, shook his head, said, "That's really nice."

"Glad you like it," I replied, "because you're probably paying for it."

That was as contentious as this divorce ever got. We went upstairs, sat down, everyone — lawyers included, it was that convivial — traded thoughts, fears, goals, concerns, worries, and hopes.

It was . . . empowering.

We hammered everything out then and there. Everything.

No egos. It was all about the kids.

They each remarried and have the kind of perfectly blended families that network TV would do a series about if *Modern Family* wasn't already taken.

Life affirming.

Career choice affirming.

5. Philosophy(s) & Psychology

I suppose some lawyers can do family law and just kind of take it as it bears ... you know, take cases as they come, don't overthink their ramifications or the fact no matter what you do you're impacting other lives in a lot of ways, some of which won't be seen or understood for years.

In other words, it may be the law, it may require brains, it may require a few other skills, but it's still, at the end of the day, a job.

That's not me. I think about . . . things. I read a lot to help me figure out those . . . things. I'm fascinated by the psychology of what I do, I'm working – and suspect I will always be – on a philosophy to help to begin to explain it all.

On top of that, I'm very – very –aware of three things that throw themselves in front of every case I'm working on: preconceptions, expectations, and assumptions.

§

Bill Dana died in 2017. His death made some news, he had a pretty lengthy obit in the *New York Times,* but there were a few other things going on news wise, so it was easy to miss. What made it even easier was the fact that Bill Dana was only moderately well known as Bill Dana. He was better known as Jose Jimenez, the character he created back in the late 1950s that, inexplicably to our 2017 sensibilities, took America by storm.

"My name ... Jose Jimenez" was *the* catchphrase of the 1960s. Just watch *The Right Stuff* for a couple of minutes – Jose is everywhere, from TVs in the background, to Alan Shepard's (Scott Glenn) constant impersonations – the most memorable as he lands on an aircraft carrier.

Bill Dana was not Hispanic. He was born in Quincy, Massachusetts in 1924 and was of Hungarian Jewish descent. His father was an immigrant, Dana grew up in a melting pot city picking up pieces of Hungarian, Italian, and Spanish. In the 1950's he got a job as a page at NBC at Rockefeller Center. He performed stand-up in his spare time, wrote jokes for other comedians – most especially for Don Adams of *Get Smart* fame – then started appearing on a number of NBC shows in the golden age of television.

He came up with the Jose Jimenez character for an appearance on the *Steve Allen Show*. It went as viral as anything could in 1959. Dana was recognized on the street, everywhere he went, as Jose Jimenez. Jose Jimenez made guest appearances on dozens of TV shows then got his own show for two years.

He was BIG. Really big. TV, lunchboxes, record albums. Then in the late '60s things began to change. Not Jose's popularity – that was always high – but the perception of the character, especially in the Hispanic community. A white guy from Quincy pretending to be a bewildered Bolivian (yup, Jose was from Bolivia, it was supposed to be part of the joke) learning the language and trying to eke out a living in the United States, was starting to be perceived as decidedly uncool.

Dana retired Jose in 1970. Actually, he killed him off and held a funeral for him on Sunset Boulevard that was attended by thousands.

So, of course, when Bill Dana died last week the headlines were all about Jose Jimenez. The rise and fall of an icon, brought down by an early form of political correctness. 'Offensive' was very prominent in many of the obits.

It would be easy – as more than a few commentators have – to assign the 2017 offensive elements of Jose Jimenez to his creator. The 'look at this guy from Massachusetts cashing in on a stereotype' jerk, pretty sad that's what it took for him to be famous.

Okay, let's stop for a minute here. Because this is what happens in life and most especially in relationships. People get caught up in the obvious, stuck in set perceptions and preconceptions that have been formed any number of ways.

That doesn't mean that they're right, it doesn't mean that they're wrong, but it almost always means that they are narrow. That necessitates stepping back and examining the whole person, the whole story.

So back to Bill Dana. Let's fill in the rest, the parts you had to read very far down the page of the obituary to find. Bill served in the infantry in Europe during WWII. He was awarded a Bronze Star. He graduated from Emerson College. He was whip smart.

He voluntarily shut down Jose in such a way that it was a resounding success with the Hispanic community. So much so that he was awarded the image award from the National Hispanic Media Coalition.

Mostly though, there's this: Dana wrote for a lot of TV Shows. He wrote what was perhaps the most iconic – and shocking for its time – TV script of the 1970s. Bill Dana wrote

the Sammy Davis Jr. episode of *All in the Family*. The one where Sammy kisses Archie in the final shot.

There was so, so much more to Bill Dana than Jose Jimenez. That's hardly unusual. When dealing with other people, especially in family law situations, it is wise and it is healthy to remember that lesson and cast preconceptions aside.

That said, I can't leave you without relaying one of Bill's greatest bits, from the *Steve Allen Show:*

"I understand you own a ranch.'
"'Yes, the name of my ranch is the Bar Nine Circle Z Rocking O
Flying W Lazy O Crazy Two Happy Seven Bar 17 Parallelogram Four
Octagon Nine Trapezoid Six Ranch.'
"'Well, do you have many cattle?'
"'No. Not many survive the branding.'"

§

Know who had probably the greatest second season in Major League Baseball history? I'll give you a hint, he played in the majors for 17 seasons, was a four-time All-Star, great fielder, and when he retired was fourth in American League history in home runs by a lefty behind Lou Gehrig, Ted Williams, and Babe Ruth.

Give up (without looking going to Baseballreference.com)? Norm Cash of the Detroit Tigers. Norm was a good fielder, a great teammate, was beloved in Detroit, finished with a lifetime .271 batting average and 377 home runs, and is largely unknown today outside of older Tiger fans.

When he is mentioned, it is usually in regard to 1961, his second year in the league. That is the year he told the pitcher/author Jim Bouton he 'wished he never had.'

Cash was 26 in 1961, coming off a really good rookie season. Good, solid, it set expectations for a good, solid, future as an above-average major league first baseman. You know, the guys that are the backbone of good teams and make the stars more, well, star-like.

Then '61 happened. Norm played in 156 games, hit .361 with 41 home runs, 132 RBIs, an astronomical WAR of 9.2, he even stole 11 bases. There were only two reasons he wasn't *the* star of baseball – Roger Maris and Mickey Mantle.

Going into the '62 season, expectations for Cash were through the roof. He crashed. He hit 118 points lower, though the home runs were still there. After '62 he settled into that 'solid but unspectacular' trend that really defined his career.

Which means, in reality, that he became one of those 'never again approached ...' guys. When he talked to Bouton about it, he was a few years from retirement, still popping away at his solid, decent pace. Still, people would say to him, "Wow, how about '61?" with more than a tinge of disappointment and wonder.

Expectations are funny things. Tough too. In law, they can be particularly ... annoying, upsetting, devastating. As a general rule, never deal with an attorney who promises a Norm Cash

1961 result. As a general rule, never be a client who expects a Norm Cash 1961 result.

As for Stormin' Norman, he was pretty comfortable in his own skin and accepted he would never be the Norm of '61.

His legacy is best summed up by his teammate and Hall of Famer, Al Kaline, "When you mention Norm Cash, I just smile."

§

A couple of things hit me recently in a particularly strange way, two seemingly unrelated things.

There was a bunch of stuff flying around about a politician/reality TV star we all know and how staff and attorneys were quitting him. A friend of mine posted a link to the 1975 Eric Carmen song *All by Myself* with a caption along the lines of 'guess who this applies to?' Good line regardless of political affiliation.

Right on top of this came the big news – a photo of Amelia Earhart sitting on a dock on an island in the South Pacific watching a Japanese freighter tow her Lockheed Electra plane away. This won the Internet. A photo showing Amelia and her navigator, Fred Noonan, after their plane went missing. Mystery solved. Well, part of the mystery, what happened to them after the Japanese took their plane was not part of the story.

The photo was hailed as groundbreaking evidence nevertheless. The guy who found it, an ex-Treasury Agent combed through the National Archives for years for overlooked Earhart evidence and turned up the photo in a box labeled 'Declassified'. He released it as proof Amelia and Fred survived and were held in the Japanese occupied Marshall Islands. A face recognition expert verified that the guy standing was Fred. Those tidbits took the Net by storm.

So, pretty cool, right?

Here's the thing(s) – there's a story behind *All by Myself*. The hook is compelling, everyone who's ever heard the song recognizes it immediately. So, do classical music fans the world over, even those well beyond Eric Carmen's reach. That's because it is based on a Rachmaninoff piece . . . down to the note. See, Eric Carmen made a perfectly reasonable assumption – he thought classical music, composer out of the 19th Century, white haired, heavily bearded, formally dressed musician long dead, copyright long expired. Again, perfectly reasonable ... and perfectly wrong.

Rachmaninoff was clean shaven, had short black hair, wore modern suits, and died in the 1930's. The copyright was held by his family. They heard the song. They sued. They won millions.

Now, about the Earhart photo. Curious thing, there are no Japanese anywhere in the photo. As anyone who has ever seen a WWII war film knows, a port under Japanese occupation would be teeming with Japanese soldiers, sailors, bureaucrats. Not a one in the picture.

Apparently, the former Treasury agent who found it was so thrilled he didn't look all that hard beyond the man, woman, and

PL-MARSHALL ISLANDS, JALUIT ATOLL, JALUIT ISLAND. ONI #14381
JALUIT HARBOR.

plane out on the barge. A Japanese military blogger, however, did. Right away. He visited the Japanese National Museum to check it out. It took him thirty minutes to find the photo there, it was from a Japanese travelogue coffee-table book published in 1935. Two years before Amelia and Fred took off on their trip around the world.

Two perfect examples of making assumptions and jumping to conclusions. The twin banes of Family Law.

§

Another problem we see a lot of from clients, judges, other lawyers… something we have to be aware of and . . . well, break free from, DOGMA … it's our enemy….

A friend of mine is doing some research for a novel that will take place during World War II. He's reading Rick Atkinson's Pulitzer Prize winning trilogy about the US Army against Germany while listening to Ian Toll's history of the War in the

Pacific while he runs. He's interested in something a little different, exploring the emotions and feel of the time, particularly 1942-43, a time he thinks Americans have lost sight — it was a time when winning the war was far, far from assured.

It was a time of uncertainty and stress and, well, everything else you can think of while Germany and Japan were running wild over most of the globe.

So, when he came across this nugget (the first of a few), he called to share, because he was pretty sure these are things that I see in my practice, for the simple reason they are just part of our DNA. He's very much in the camp of "the past isn't dead, it isn't even past," so ...

The Zero. The Japanese designed and built the Zero, the finest fighter in the world when it came out in 1940, almost totally off the grid. Not only did no one in the West know the Japanese were building an air force comprised of planes of their own design, they doubted that the Japanese could do more than take off and land. "The Japanese are physiologically unsuited to be pilots." "The only planes they can build are cheap imitations of our 'real' planes," and more was the dogma of the day.

Then the Zero came out in August 1940. It made its debut in China. It could out climb and out maneuver any plane in the world ... and it packed a punch. Through the rest of 1940 and through 1941 Zeros cleared the skies of everything the Chinese flew, including the U.S. volunteers flying for Claire Chennault's Flying Tigers. In that time not a single Zero was shot down in aerial combat. That is not a misprint.

General Chennault was impressed. He issued orders to his pilots, "Never ~ never ~ dogfight a Zero. Always fly in pairs, never get separated."

As importantly, he sent detailed intelligence reports to Washington on the Japanese's amazing new weapon. In-depth discussions on the Zero's specs and what could be done to stop them from shooting down everything that flew.

All things that, when adopted, led to the end of Zeros ruling the skies. Unfortunately, they were independently adopted months after Pearl Harbor after the death of hundreds of pilots and the loss of hundreds of planes ~ Chennault's reports and analysis and recommendations had been tossed. They hadn't supported current dogma and no one in the peacetime military was remotely interested in rocking the boat.

So, yeah, dogma. Strict adherence to a belief system in total disregard for changing facts and conditions. It is the enemy in family law. It's certainly the enemy in mediation.

There's a flip side to this bit of history. Remember that 18 month period where not a single Zero was shot down? Turns out that was a problem. Great machines, revolutionary in fact, but not tested through months and months of service. The

Japanese did not discover their flaws — lack of armor, no self-sealing fuel tanks, the inability to take any kind of combat punishment — until it was too late.

To paraphrase Hemingway, it's the hits that make us strong.

§

In family law, nostalgia for the 'good times' is, quite simply a killer.

The NFL version of the Baltimore Colts came into existence in 1953. They played at Memorial Stadium smack dab in the middle of a sprawling working-class neighborhood.

Playing in the NFL in the early 1950s barely provided a living for most players, so they worked regular jobs around practices and games and throughout the off season. Those early Colts settled in the neighborhoods around the park and ended up working alongside their fans.

The Colts weren't good. Their first four years they struggled to win five games, never sniffed the playoffs. But their games sold well, at the very least a Colt fan could go to Stadium to support the players they knew while watching the 'big boys' like the Cleveland Browns and Detroit Lions come in (boy, have things changed).

Things changed in 1956 though, and in a big way. The woeful Pittsburgh Steelers cut their fourth string quarterback, the Colts gave him a tryout and signed Johnny Unitas. In 1957 Unitas became the starting quarterback and the Colts had their first winning season.

The next year they won the NFL Championship in the game that changed the NFL's fortunes forever – national television, the largest television audience of all time, Yankee Stadium against the Giants, the first overtime game ... ever.

The Colts became good . . . very, very good. Their stars, Unitas, Raymond Berry, Big Daddy Liscomb, Tom Matte, Alan Ameche, Lenny Moore, many, many more were legends. Legends who lived in the same neighborhoods as their fans, walked to practice and games at Municipal Stadium, drank in the same bars, worked alongside them. Johnny Unitas was the face of the NFL by 1958 yet worked in a welding shop in the neighborhood.

Colt fans weren't really fans – they were a part of it all. A Sunday night after a game (only Sundays back then), in the bar on the corner, anyone who cared to could ask Unitas why he called *that* play, or Liscomb what it was like to sack Y.A. Title. It's not surprising, then, that Colt fans were devoted. The Baltimore Colt Marching Band, composed solely of fans, walked to games, gained fame of their own, in a homegrown sort of way.

The scene in *Diner* where a character won't commit to marrying his girlfriend unless she passes a test about the Colts was not much of a stretch for the writer/director Barry Levinson, a Baltimore native and die-hard Colt fan. It rang true.

The Colts were good for the better part of the next 20 years, then they just got bad. They, infamously, traded Unitas to the

San Diego Chargers, and went south from there. Still, though, their fans stuck with them and the band still marched to games.

Then, after the 1983 season, the Colt's owner packed everything up in the middle of the night and escaped to Indianapolis.

Baltimore was crushed. The band stuck together, for a while people still went to the stadium on Sundays (if the Orioles weren't playing) and sat in the stands while the band played.

Baltimore wanted the team back and never stopped working to do so. Finally, in 1996, they got their team. Art Modell ironically abandoned Cleveland and moved the Browns to Baltimore ... where they were quickly renamed the Ravens.

All was well again. They even won a Super Bowl in 2000.

For everyone who grew up in the '50s, '60s, and (very) early '70s it was . . . Not remotely the same.

The Ravens play in a new stadium in the Inner Harbor, downtown Baltimore. There are no local neighborhoods. Even if there were, players in the '90s and 2000s, no matter what position they play, have no need for a second or off-season job. Players aren't walking to the stadium. The band had to change its name to the Ravens Marching Band, but they don't march much anymore ~ certainly not from home to the stadium. No regular Baltimorean ever had a beer with Ray Lewis, Joe Flacco, et. al.

Johnny Unitas' Colt passing records were all officially broken ~ by Peyton Manning playing 589 miles from Municipal Stadium. As of 2014, the Colts had played more seasons in Indianapolis than they had in Baltimore.

Those Baltimore fans – the real Colt fans – were nostalgic for a time that, over a few years of no football, was made better by receding into the past. As such (and of course) it could never be recreated. The Ravens were fine, but they were never going to be the Colts. Baltimore in 1996 wasn't the Baltimore of 1966, the NFL of the 2000s is almost unrecognizable from the game played that night in Yankee Stadium in 1957.

Baltimore was nostalgic for a time, a place, people that could never be replicated. Those fans still pining for Barry Levinson's Baltimore weren't happy, those Colt fans who took the Ravens and the new for what is was ... well, they enjoyed it. Chief among the latter, by the way, was Johnny Unitas.

Nostalgia, in small measure, is nice. In family law, it can be a hindrance. Think about it.

§

Being a grown up is essential.

I have a friend who recently took a run through the Gettysburg battlefield while doing some research. He took this picture there.

Gettysburg, he relates, is an eclectic experience: peaceful, evocative, serene, haunting, bewildering in a 'what made them do this' sort of way, fascinating, somber, bucolic . . . . occasionally annoyingly kitschy, overbearing, celebratory where it most definitely should not be.

He's referring not to the gift and antique shops that crowd the edges of the park vying for space with fast food restaurants and cheap hotels, but to the monuments that litter chunks of the fields.

Gettysburg has some overwhelming, incongruous, baroque monuments, many of which shatter sight lines and loom over the visitor. If it looks as if there were a competition among the states to outdo each other in honoring (or exaggerating) their contribution/sacrifice at the worst battle ever fought in the Americas, it is because there most certainly was.

There is, however, a remarkable exception. It is tucked away in a corner of the Wheatfield, scene of a vicious, incredibly brutal, afternoon long fight on July 2nd, 1863, that eviscerated a Union Corps and where the Confederacy came within a hairsbreadth of breaking the Union line. It is nestled in a copse of trees in a still, quiet, sun dabbled section of field a little bit off the usual visitor's trek and well away from traffic.

The Irish Brigade Monument. By July 1863, the Irish Brigade, a potent Union fighting force, had been bled white. The Wheatfield ended them. Even at first glance, the monument is visceral. A bronze and green granite Celtic Cross curled around the base is a sleeping, life-sized bronze Irish Wolfhound.

Here's the neat thing about this, I think, and a lesson for everyone who's ever been in conflict with another person for when the conflict is over: the sculptor chosen by the state of New York, Rudolph O'Donovan was well-known, Irish, and specifically requested by the survivors of the brigade.

He was very much touched and honored to be asked to create something for a group of men he admired. O'Donovan was also at Gettysburg on July 2nd. He was an artillery man in the Confederate Army directly across from the Irish Brigade.

Just saying, adults move on.

§

And, to move on, you have to get over it.

Netflix has a six-part documentary by the estimable Errol Morris called *Wormwood*. It's been critically acclaimed, justifiably I think, though I thought at one point that it may have been an episode too long. But I've changed my mind on that, for reasons you'll read below.

Wormwood is about the 1953 death of Frank Olsen in Manhattan. He 'fell' out of a 13th floor window at the Stadler Hotel. The family was told he had committed suicide. His  employer reported that he had seemed depressed and upset and had recommended he seek counseling – which is why Frank was in New York to begin with. Frank's employer was the United States Government. Frank was an army scientist who worked at Fort Detrick, Maryland, on the U.S. biological weapon program.

Frank Olsen left a wife and three young children.

There things stood until the 1970's when, in the aftermath of Watergate, Nelson Rockefeller was tasked with investigating the CIA. In the course of the Congressional hearings it emerged, quite unexpectedly, that Frank Olsen worked for the CIA and had been unwillingly given LSD, repeatedly, as part of an experiment gone badly wrong. Frank's suicide was directly attributed to the drug.

In a stunningly groundbreaking move, the government admitted its mistake. President Ford apologized to the family in the Oval Office. They were invited to address the Congressional Hearings and they were compensated $750,000 for the wrongful death of Frank Olsen.

So, as happy an ending as one could have hoped, right? Wrong, because despite the government's admissions and the compensation, Frank's son, Eric, who had harbored questions about his father's death for years even while having very hazy memories of him, dove deeper still into it.

The rest of the documentary traces Eric's 'search for the truth.' Eric is a constant presence throughout the documentary and it's impossible not to be incredibly impressed by his obvious intelligence, erudition, and research.

For a while, at least. He raises the possibility that his father was murdered. Some very competent lawyers join his 'quest' and the Pulitzer Prize winning journalist Seymour Hersh pitches in. New facts are uncovered. New theories abound.

It's somewhere in this part of the documentary that you start to notice a few things. Eric went to Harvard, stayed for postgraduate studies and was developing his own theory of psychotherapy that looked impressive. But he walked away after the Congressional hearings. He seemed to walk away from everything. His entire existence revolved around 'getting at the truth.' He's the reason the story extends past the 1970's and is still going strong.

Eric was obsessed. It becomes equally as clear that the people who are helping him, the lawyers, the New York Attorney General's office, Hersh, are trying to tell him, without doing it directly, to let it go. Let it go, and, implicitly, get a life.

" Bonh jaws, like conrmons shears, bit the craft completely in twain."

—*Page 500.*

At the end, the only one who puts it to him straight is Errol Morris, he asks him the question on camera. Eric replies, "I feel like I've let it go. But it hasn't let me go."

In the end, it seemed to me the entire show was really about Eric's obsession. And that not only struck me as sad but struck a chord as well.

In family law, at some point for everyone involved, the healthy, 'get on with your life live long and prosper moment' is the moment you let it go. It's done. That moment is hopefully long·before Eric's moment (if it ever comes) and before the whale gets you, as Captain Ahab would surely attest.

§

I started thinking about this way back before the first Presidential debate in 2016. Way back in the primordial mists, before even Alec Baldwin entered the fray.

The good old days. I decided to explore the concept of 'Mansplaining' – you know, the inability of some (even some running for higher office) to listen to … anyone. Which is bad enough except that by the rules of Mansplaining (there are rules, right?), that inability to listen is followed, almost without pause, by the compulsion to expound. Endlessly. The rule of thumb seems to be: the less one knows, the harder and longer one explains.

I thought 'mansplaining' was a neat word even while, as evidenced by recent events and explanations of unexplainable acts and behaviors, I never thought it was necessarily practiced by only one gender. Just a good, solid word that explained much about the level of discourse in the U.S. right now.

I considered this post a little too long and before I knew it the second debate was looming. Then, of course, it really hit the fan and, well, a few days of non-stop, at times deranged, mansplaining. I wasn't exactly sure what direction to go in – there were more than a few to attack, but they seemed so …too…very … strident.

It all coalesced, though, while I was flipping through the NFL and MLB pregame shows Sunday. Then it came to me, the missing piece, the Rosetta Stone of business, political, interpersonal verbal conflict in the 2010's – it's all Madden NFL'92's fault. Okay, not just Madden NFL '92. Madden '92 and the 24 versions since.

You may remember Madden NFL '92, it had so-so graphics, bad music, worse sound effects, and was pretty easy to beat after some repetition. But, it was *FOOTBALL*. Pro Football, and it wasn't a stupid knob-controlled arcade game. You had to call plays. Pick from a list of cool sounding, seemingly ripped from the playbooks of Bill Parcells, real football plays.

Of course, all anyone really needed to win was to take the Detroit Lions and give the ball to Barry Sanders. He was unstoppable.

It was fun. Flashy and fun. Playing it gave a glimpse into what it took to call plays in an NFL game. Remember, by the way, that this was before the heyday of fantasy football. Back then fantasy football was an arcane paper and pencil (and lots of erasers) game played by groups of friends pouring over newspapers to find statistics every week. In the primitive Internet Age, it took real dedication. Madden NFL seemed a nice side dish for it.

Over the years, Madden's graphics improved to the point where they rival the real thing; the play lists for offense and defense have lengthened considerably; there's much more control over the players; the music is better; there's the running commentary from real TV announcers.

Madden NFL'16 is the 24th edition of the game. That's 24 years and a few generations that have played it and now buy the new version the second it comes out every year. They've seen both games evolve – Madden and the real NFL. A funny thing

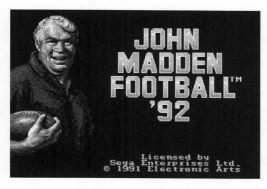

has happened along the way, as has been commented on by Jay Kang of the *New York Times* (among others): a lot of the people who have been playing Madden NFL over the years think they are football experts.

If you step back and look at it, it makes some weird sense. The game has all the bells, whistles, uses all the neat NFL nomenclature and gives the appearance of complexity. More than anything, it invites players to believe it's the real thing. But, it's not. Not when compared to actually coaching an NFL team. Any NFL team.

Moreover, in Madden NFL'17, the person with the controller controls every aspect of the game. Nothing real intrudes on this omnipotence – weather, injuries, emotions, adapting to what the other team's doing. To paraphrase Marcia Gay Harden in *Millers Crossing*: 'that's Madden NFL all over, no heart.'

I mean, there's a reason the NFL has assistant coaches to the assistant coaches, all with their own specialties. Love it, hate it, ignore it, but there's no getting away from the fact that coaching in the NFL is amazingly complex. It's not 'land a man on the moon complex' but it's not that far off and they share the same technology today.

Madden NFL'17 has come a long, long way. And it has changed beyond the graphics – now it's impossible to stop Brady to Gronkowski.

None of this stops lifelong Madden players from flooding the radio-waves; they know, they've experienced the game. They talk over each other, hosts, and most especially, anyone they're pretty sure never played football above peewee.

Normally, it's annoying but harmless. Like when your brother-in-law erupts half-way through Thanksgiving dinner and explains in excruciating detail why the Lions coaches should be fired en masse. Or, why the Cowboys used the wrong blitz

package because he won his local Madden championship back in '09 on exactly the same play when he used a package no one would have expected and it would have worked now if only Jason Garrett had gone to a real football school instead ..." (That would be Princeton, but to tell him that would invite a discourse on the intellectual elite.)

Again, annoying but harmless. But, when the same brother-in-law fills you in on everything he infers you're doing wrong with your divorce, then tells you all about the custody case you have ... or the custody case you don't have, it is no longer harmless.

Look, I loved Cliff Clavin as much as anyone. When he was the lone voice at the back of the bar. Now the bar's full of Cliff Clavins fueled by Madden and the Internet and the detritus of the Information Age. All I'm saying is, ignore the Clavins aside from their admittedly high-amusement value and, when something matters, go to the source material.

§

There's a certain behavior I see on a fairly consistent basis in my practice. It occurs at that point where someone in mediation has to – I mean, has to – cede a position and move on and they do. But can't leave it be.

You know the type – they've agreed, made a point of making sure everybody knows how very much they turned themselves inside out to be so magnanimous, then bring it up time and time again, but usually in the context of, "Well, I had to do that, the rules were against me, it's not fair, but the system's rigged for (their particular circumstance goes here.)"

This stuff is everywhere now. It seems to have snuck into popular consciousness sometime over the last few years. Football coaches who complain that the other team 'broke the spirit of the rules' but not the actual rule, as if there are two separate rule books. Baseball pitchers who lost 9-1 but ascribe it to the umpire's 'tight strike zone.' Politicians of every stripe embracing the rules when they win but bitterly grousing about how the system is rigged the minute they fall behind.

A loss is never a loss. Giving up something in negotiations is never being smart or doing the right thing to resolve an issue it's 'I was forced', 'had no choice', 'the system sucks, dude.'

The effects of this linger. In my professional life it means hard feelings and a tougher end game for everyone and, when children are involved, acrimony that will not be shielded from the child. Said long and loud enough and it becomes self-perpetuating: "Gee, the only reason I see dad every other week is because the system's rigged, dude."

In politics, it means candidates moaning and crying and doing real damage to their parties. The Democrats, the GOP, doesn't matter, regardless of the results, as long as there is someone or some nebulous 'thing' out there to blame, no one thinks of their party. That they aren't thinking about the United States and you and me is implicit.

 Which brings me, quite logically, to *Mad Max: Fury Road*. Zipping right past the great acting, the effects, the plot, the strong female character, and all the other things that put it on everyone's top ten list and got it nominated for ten Oscars, I was struck – really struck – by a series of quiet moments.

No real dialogue, certainly no long explanations, and yet so much was conveyed. Not giving anything away for those who still have *Mad Max: Fury Road* queued up (watch it!), this is a story where people who don't know each other are violently thrown together. They have to decide in an instant whether to work together or kill each other.

The film is full of small moments where a look passes between characters – the most poignant is between Charlize Theron and Tom Hardy in the middle of a high-octane chase. They look; they take mental inventory; they decide to work together. After that the trust is pretty implicit.

This happens over and over again, is never expounded upon, just those simple looks. Not everything goes well – some things completely fall apart – and yet there are no recriminations, indeed, it's just accepted as the cost of … well, you'll see.

There are certainly no excuses, whining, or what ifs. And despite all, no one complains about the system. They're too busy worrying about the welfare of the others.

Here's hoping I don't have to wait for the apocalypse to see this first hand in practice.

6. Strategy

I negotiate all day every day. You probably do too, no matter what you do. Life is about negotiations – after all, the social contract is a contract, and contracts have to be negotiated.

Negotiation and strategy, obviously, go hand in hand. Even – or maybe especially – in what should be the non-zero-sum game of mediation.

My thoughts about strategy:

§

First, foremost, most importantly, strategy and tactics (they are separate, see below) are one-hundred percent, absolutely, completely (get the picture) dependent on communication between client and attorney.

There's a Saturday Night Live skit from 1986 called One More Mission; It is really one of the great SNL bits of all time. (Right up there with the real ending of *It's a Wonderful Life*).

One More Mission perfectly – *Perfectly* – sums up a chunk of what I do on a daily basis. Jon Lovitz is a 1940's movie studio mogul and the late, irreplaceable, Phil Hartman is a washed-up star. A bit of it goes like this:

Johnny O'Connor (Phil Hartman): [reflecting] Maybe I've made too many of these war movies. Maybe I should take a

rest, huh, Harry?

Harry (John Lovitz): Well, I'm glad you brought that up, Johnny ... I was thinking you should take a rest, too. A permanent one.

Johnny O'Connor: [confused] What do you mean?

Harry: I'm letting you go.

Johnny O'Connor: You mean...?

Harry: Yes. Your contract isn't being renewed.

Johnny O'Connor: But, Harry, I...

Harry: You're **finished,** Johnny!

Johnny O'Connor: Don't mince words!

Harry: I think you stink!

Johnny O'Connor: Listen, Harry, if you're unhappy with my work, tell me now!

Harry: You're **through,** do you hear me, **through!** You'll never work in this town again!

Johnny O'Connor: Don't leave me hanging by a thread! Let me know how I stand!

Harry: I think you're the **worst** actor I've ever seen, and I get five hundred letters a day telling me the same!

Johnny O'Connor: What's the word on the street?

It's very funny on several levels. But, of course, it hits home for me on a professional level because I deal in communication. It's my medium. There are many layers, different circumstances, a hundred variables but it may just come down to these combinations: Lawyer (me) with client; client with spouse; lawyer (me again) with spouse's lawyer.

Sometimes my conversations are virtually identical to the one above. Not so amusing, then.

But, here's the important thing, the thing I try to impart to my clients – this kind of active non-hearing is not because the other guy is stupid, or dull, or just doesn't get it.

It occurs because it usually involves some fact or 'truth' no one wants to face on a good day, never mind in the middle of a divorce. Like Johnny not wanting to face the end of his acting career.

My job is to get people through this. From any angle.

§

There's a show on NBC called *Timeless*. Apparently, it's doing pretty well. It's about a criminal who steals a top-secret government time machine and, of course, zips back in time to change things toward his own ends. Well, maybe. Whatever he's doing (the NBC promos refer to him with the ever ambiguous 'mysterious thief') he's zipping back to famous events and trying to change them for ... well, who the hell knows.

The first episode had him saving the Hindenburg, then blowing it up; in the second he's trying to make sure that John Wilkes Booth and his band of assorted nut-jobs complete their original plan – kill Lincoln, Grant, and the leaders of the government. Why? Who knows?

Chasing the mystery man is a historian who just happens to be handsome, a sort of SEAL/Delta Team guy with a heart, and an African-American scientist. They promise to do so through several seasons while saving history at the last second and ... well, whatever.

My lack of enthusiasm in the show revolves around a plot device. Early on the historian asks bad guy, "Why are you doing all this?"

Bad guy replies, "I'm just following your book."

"I haven't written a book," historian says with furrowed brow.

"You will," Bad guy answers knowingly and shows her a nice, thick notebook – in her handwriting.

"Give that to me!" Historian shrieks.

"No," Bad guy solemnly replies, "all in due time."

And .... that was it for me. I mean, the bad guy (who the show just telegraphed isn't really that bad) isn't showing her the notebook because it means the series would end. It'd be a made-for-TV-movie and done in ninety minutes. Instead, the show's writers are going to drag the viewers through a few seasons of teases, red herrings, blind alleys and really crappy history (for a show about history, it's really pretty shaky on the subject) because the two main characters can't be bothered to talk to each other.

The late, great Roger Ebert used to compile a list of movie devices. Like:

*"**Idiot Plot:** Any plot containing problems that would be solved instantly if all of the characters were not idiots."*

This isn't quite an idiot plot, but it is a variation – a story that exists solely because of inexcusable, irrational, lack of communication.

It's ridiculous in a TV show. It's sad when it comes to divorce and mediation and pretty much anything revolving around family. Just saying.

If the plot of a run of the mill TV show can't support the lack of communication between characters, imagine the effect a similar lack of communication has on your lawyer......

§

We all know the story of the Gordian Knot – the impossible puzzle that baffled the greatest minds of the Ancient World until Alexander the Great employed one of the first life-hacks ever recorded and cut it with his sword.

When the story's told that way, the inference is clear – direct action is the most effective action. You know, as a man of action, world conqueror, Alexander couldn't be bothered with the niceties of an intricate intellectual puzzle.

Well, maybe. First – here's what the Gordian Knot was: way back, long before Alexander, Telmessus, a city in what is now central Turkey was without a king. An oracle (this is a Greek Myth – there's always an oracle) decreed that the next man to enter the city in an ox-cart would be king. Enter Gordias, a

farmer. He undoubtedly was coming to town to sell some fresh produce, he had the good fortune to do so on an ox-cart. He was immediately declared king. His son, Midas (yes, that Midas), was so pleased to find himself suddenly a prince, dedicated the cart to Zeus and tied the cart's yoke to a post with 'the knot.'

The problem was legendary, the first person who could find the two ends of the knot would be the first person to solve it. Another Oracle predicted that whoever did so would rule Asia. Or have many military victories. Or a hundred other rewards. It's hazy.

Or it was until Alexander the Great came along during one of his campaigns. Once he solved the problem, it was definitely 'rule Asia.'

So, Alexander hacked through the knot and picked up both ends and won. Except, he almost certainly did no such thing. Alexander was a student – a good student – of Aristotle and as such he employed a much more subtle solution.

He pulled the linchpin of the yoke out, then pulled the yoke off the post and the knot fell out. Done. He did pretty well for himself for years after until, as Hans Gruber tells us, he wept for having no more worlds to conquer.

Alexander's real solution to an unsolvable problem has been emulated in fiction through the ages. Think Captain Kirk's solution to the no-win Kobayashi Maru scenario (he changed the computer program). Better yet, Steve Rogers. He got the opportunity to become Captain America because he directly emulated Alexander – if you remember the (first) movie, you'll remember the greased flagpole problem.

In psychology there's something called the elegant solution. There's a few different definitions, needless to say none of them included slashing at the problem with a sword. The best definition: The solution to a problem with the minimum effort to produce the best result.

That's mediation when it's done right.

§

I fulfilled a wish-list item and finally saw the San Francisco Giants play in their beautiful stadium. Fun night even though the Giants were going nowhere. Somewhere along the line, I was reminded of this story – I think it serves as a pretty good metaphor for opting for mediation over litigation and how we at Triangle Smart Divorce do things .... or, maybe it's just me and the breeze off of the Bay ...

There are several versions of this story – I choose to believe this one. Sometime during the 1955 or '56 season the Yankees brought up a nineteen-year-old shortstop. The Yankees had just won 7 pennants and 6 World Series in 8 years. The kid, however, was hardly cowered by all that, he was cocky and irritating.

His chief target was, incredibly enough, Mickey Mantle. Mantle had come up as a 19-year-old shortstop in 1950 renowned for his power and speed. Mantle was timed at 3.1 seconds to first base, the fastest ever recorded. The rookie wanted to race him claiming he was faster.

By the mid-'50's Mantle was still fast but had suffered a series of leg injuries, the most famous one in the 1951 World Series. He didn't want to race but, like an aging gunfighter in the Old West, he felt he had to accept the challenge.

After weeks of listening to the rookie's claims, Mantle finally walked up to him in Kansas City and said they'd race. It was 100 degrees out. They marked out forty yards in the outfield.

The rest of the Yankees came out to watch. And bet. Against the rookie. The rookie jogged to the starting line and said, "Okay, let's go."

Mantle shook his head, "Not so fast, how do I know you're fast? I only have your word for it."

The kid was flummoxed. Mantle said, "First, you have to beat Bauer." Hank Bauer, 33-year-old outfielder, Marine veteran of Okinawa. And he looked it. The kid readily agreed. What he didn't know was that Bauer was still one of the quickest Yankees. The kid won but had to bust it the last twenty yards to do it.

Slightly winded he reported back to the starting line where Mantle was waiting with pitcher Don Larson (of World Series perfect game fame). "Gee kid," Mantle said, "you beat an old man – guy was wounded in the war for Christ sakes, didn't tell me anything – you want to race me, you gotta beat Don here, you know, someone closer to our age."

The rookie agreed (he had no choice with the rest of the Yankees watching and hollering), completely unaware that Larson, a great athlete, was the second fastest guy on the team. The kid beat him by a few feet.

Sweating, breathing heavily, the kid went back to the starting line where Mantle was waiting with Yogi Berra. "Wow, you beat a pitcher, big deal," Mantle said, "beat Yogi and we'll race."

The kid looked at Yogi – stocky, short-legged, and a *catcher* – and readily agreed. The kid hadn't been in the Big Leagues long enough, in the era before televised games every day, to know that Berra was one of the quickest players in baseball. The kid beat him by a whisker.

Drenched in sweat and panting he walked to the finish line to find a fresh Mantle in a crouch, "Nice job, ready ...one, two, three go," and he blew him away. The kid was barely able to finish in the heat.

Love this story ... and I think it's a pretty good representation of what we do at Triangle Smart Divorce. We plan ahead. Way ahead.

§

Do a Google search right now – this second – for Billy Mitchell and you'll pull up about five pages on a controversy of staggering consequence: did a video game player really set the all-time score in Donkey Kong or did he rig the game? Really.

There's another Billy Mitchell, just a tad more famous, though he's getting a little more obscure everyday. I suppose the reasons are obvious, him having died before the advent of video games. Frankly, I only thought of him because a little while back, I was at a week-long seminar for lawyers in Chantilly, Virginia and ran across his statue.

It was in the new Smithsonian Air Space Museum, about a mile from our hotel. That's it to the right, Billy Mitchell, the plane in the background was the Spad XVI he flew– famously –

in World War I. His statue is not there because he was a war hero, it's there because he lost a court case in 1925, the first 'Trial of the Century' for the 20th.

Billy Mitchell was a lot of things, almost all astounding. A great pilot, fantastic organizer and leader, he planned and led the

Allied Air offenses of September 1918. He came back to the US a hero. He came back with a lot of hard-earned beliefs, almost none of which were shared by his contemporaries, especially those safely behind the lines.

He believed that air power was the future. He believed that the battleship was dead, aircraft carriers were essential, planes were the key to protecting US territories, bombers could sink ships, and Japan was a major threat to American interests in the Pacific.

He proved the bit about a plane's ability to sink ships in 1921, despite the Navy's protests and outright cheating. Almost no one else took much else of what he said seriously except, ironically, the Japanese. Mitchell was a Cassandra, he was a decade, at least, ahead of his time. The one thing he did learn in those early post-war years was something every Cassandra eventually finds out– no one likes them.

Mitchell's was a privileged background– he was from a wealthy Wisconsin railroad and banking family, his father was a US senator, he grew up in France, and graduated from George Washington University.

In short, he was someone who was used to being heard. He was, to vastly understate, loud and opinionated about what he believed.

As a pilot, he was in the forefront of aviation safety in primitive days. He warned about safety issues loudly and

continuously. Again, he was usually ignored. He did, however, mange to infuriate the Army brass, the Navy as a whole, future President Franklin Delano Roosevelt, and President Coolidge.

When the Navy's first rigid airship *Shenandoah* crashed in a storm in September 1925, killing 14 of her crew, Mitchell exploded. He accused the Army, Navy and War Department of gross incompetence while throwing out the 'T' word – treason. He didn't say it to a few friends or colleagues at an officer's club, he said to the newspapers and radio. The quotes spread around the country like wildfire.

He was court martialed. It was said that the order came straight from Coolidge. Eight charges, all wrapped around criticizing his superiors. The defense brought in 90 witnesses, some famous, to testify that Mitchell was right, that everything he said was on the nose correct and if only the Army and Navy listened to him. The trial, though, wasn't about him being right, it was about the insubordination.

The trial made for a terrific movie 1955's *The Court Martial of Billy Mitchell* starring Gary Cooper, and it transfixed the nation back in December, 1925, but the verdict was never in doubt.

Mitchell was guilty of gross insubordination. Mitchell was suspended from the Army on no pay for five years. He resigned rather than accept the sentence. Without his uniform, Mitchell found that his influence over all matters regarding the air was nil.

From the movie, unfortunately, Billy Mitchell's best friend wasn't Steve McGarrett and he definitely wasn't married to Samantha Stevens

So, here's the thing, something we try to impart to our clients — it's great to be right about things but being right is almost never an end all thing. Especially with legal issues.

Billy Mitchell's rank of Brigadier General was eventually restored. He is the only individual to have a military plane named after him. The main dining hall at GWU is named in his honor. An act of Congress promoted him to Major General and the statue was placed in the Air-Space Museum.

All years after his death.

That's all great, now. But there is a very solid case to be made (books have been written about this) that had Mitchell not been court martialed and had figured out somewhere along the road how to play the diplomacy game instead of the bull in the china store gambit, he and the United States would have been infinitely better off – he might have been listened to.

If you doubt that, there's this: in the early 1920's Mitchell warned that an aircraft assault on Pearl Harbor was the logical place for an air strike to cripple the US Pacific fleet.

§

Here's a story from Ireland and a pretty good metaphor for staying on top of things.

I have a friend who toured Ireland with his rugby team in the late '80's. After he played against the Dublin Wanderers, they gave him and his teammates passes to the All-Ireland Hurling Finals the next day. That's basically the Irish Super Bowl.

If you haven't been exposed to hurling, it's . . . well, insane. My friend's description, by the way. When a rugby player calls a sport insane, it's got to be crazy.

Hurling is an ancient sport, was banned by the British as being too Irish, though, really, if they had allowed everyone in Ireland to play it, I've got to think they would have had an easier time there.

Hurling is a combination of field hockey, lacrosse, baseball, rugby, and ice hockey. It's played with solid wood sticks; the ball is as hard as a baseball. The object of the game is to hit the ball into a soccer-like goal (3 points), or through rugby-like goal posts (1 point). Hockey-like checking, if not full tackling, is allowed.

Players wear shorts, cleats, colorful shirts, optional light helmets, and mouth guards. No shoulder pads, no Kevlar.

The scariest thing in a game full of scary things is that players can flip the ball up in the air and smack it like a baseball coach hitting fungoes. They do this, though, while sprinting and with defenders draped over them.

The game was fantastic, the crowd trading songs, county flags flying, Guinness flowing, there were some injuries, about as many as you'd see in a rugby match. None serious. No one died. Which was amazing.

After the game, my friend and his teammates were allowed down on the pitch and got to chat with some of the bruised, battered, and somewhat bloodied players.

His first question was obvious, "How do you not get killed?"

The answer was as pragmatic as it was practiced, "If you stay in top shape and stick with the play, close to the man you're marking, you can't get really hurt . . . by the stick."

If you think about it, as my friend certainly did, it's simple physics. If you're right on top of the guy swinging for the fences the stick will barely sting – it just hasn't traveled very far.

If, however, you're an arm or stick length away when someone swings, you get the full force of the stick ... if you're another step off, you risk getting nailed by a rock-hard ball at 80 mph.

While my friend processed that, he was looking around the pitch and was struck by something. Unlike rugby, where men and women played at high levels into their 40s, there were no elder statesmen to be found. There didn't seem to be more than a couple over thirty.

No Peyton Manning getting a last shot at a championship.

He mentioned it to his very patient new friend. The man from Galway laughed, "There are no old hurlers, ya' got to know when to walk away from this sport."

"Which is when?"

"When you lose a step and you're a second late when you never were before. That's it, you go play soccer."

I'm sure you probably see where I'm going with this. When you're engaged in a family law matter, give it your all, stick close to the issues, stay on top of the process, and know when to get out.

§

Europeans in the 16th Century were obsessed with the 'New World.' And why not, America was the great unknown, the land of unseen wonders, unknown peoples and animals. Books and pamphlets about the Americas were the viral media of the day. They were read and passed around with voracity.

So, it came to pass in the 1570s that the informed Englishman knew that the wilderness known as Florida was populated by unicorns, lions, and dragons.

This was due to the writings of Sir John Hawkins, an English sailor (and slave trader and privateer and hero of the defeat of the Armada and a dozen other things, multi-tasking being a real thing back then).

Sir John was a lot of things, but he was certainly no Captain Cook or Charles Darwin. He was a sailor, soldier, capitalist, killer, navigator, slaver, royal suck up ... in other words, not the guy anyone would expect to come back from a yearlong cruise to Central and North America with solid observations about culture and nature.

Which he didn't, of course. Hawkins skirted the coast of Florida very briefly as he was fleeing the Spanish after a military disaster – the 1570s equivalent to an airport layover. In one of his brief stays along the coast he ran into a group of natives wearing necklaces of large animal horns. They didn't look like any animal horns he had ever seen so he assumed they were from unicorns, another animal he had never seen.

At the time, there was a theory that 'no beast could exist in nature without its natural enemy.' Everyone knew that lions were the natural enemies of unicorns, therefore, there had to be lions in Florida.

When he returned to England, Hawkins published his tales supplemented by a crew member's story of catching a dragon with a fishing rod using a dog as bait. (That sounds stupid but considering the abundance of alligators in Florida it has a lot more credence than the unicorn thing).

It wasn't long before informed Europeans filled in uninformed Europeans about the unicorns, lions, and dragons in the Florida swamps and soon everybody was talking to everybody else about the Florida unicorns.

A false observation led to a false conclusion led to false knowledge, shared over and over again until it became accepted as truth and was shared some more.

I think I have just described most Internet stories about family law. (Okay, a lot more than that, but I am a family law attorney trying to make a specific point). Posts, blogs, stories about divorce, custody, alimony, etc., are viewed and shared over and over again. The point is, though, that unless we know what the original author was looking at when they started, we can't know how valid their conclusions are.

Did they see the necklace from afar, or did they walk over to the person wearing it, look closely, and ask where the horns came from?

§

Who are you negotiating with? Practically everyone you meet.

And people have their own desires, needs, and agendas. And as a coping mechanism, their subconscious more often protects them by throwing up terror barriers to make them retreat to places that are known, safe and familiar.

When this is going on, you can't reason with them, you can't plead with them, and you can't argue with them...nothing gets through.

To get through you have to change your approach and break through the walls they've placed to avoid getting hurt or controlled.

The brain has three parts. They usually work together but tend to pull apart in times of stress:

"Snake brain"—fight or flight—reacting and not thinking

"Limbic brain"—powerful feelings, like love, joy, anger, sadness

"Primate brain"—logic & reason; collects data; analyzes & makes decision

When things get 'hairy,' the Amygdala—small area deep in your brain which senses a threat and flies into action – hijacks; the brain and directs impulses to or diverts from the frontal cortex (that would be the logical part of your brain).

Like water on a stove it can simmer and you can function. But when it hits rapid boil, then it's over— the ability to reason drops, working memory fails, and stress hormones flood everything. This is the place where it's a pretty good idea to try and intervene – it can be done – before your brain is hijacked and you are entirely at its mercy.

It should be noted that there are these things called 'mirror neurons' that we all have, they are exactly what they sound like, they allow (force?) us to mirror another's actions in your mind. Everyone hungers to be mirrored. Everyone feels a deficit when they aren't.

These techniques work with your coworkers, your spouse, your friends, your children, your boss, your clients, your sales prospects and more. BUT they may be unlikely to work with bullies and jerks.

Thanks to Mark Goulston and his book *Just Listen*, here are the steps I now ask clients to try to go through during the divorce process, particularly when we are pursuing settlement as the solution:

Go …
From resisting to listening
From listening to considering
From considering to willing to do
From willing to do to doing
From doing to glad they did …
… then continue

§

My nine rules for taking control of a stressful situation, also adopted from *Just Listen*:

Get your own emotions under control first

Learn to listen without a filter (no conclusions, no formed perceptions)

Put yourself in the other person's shoes and make them feel "felt"

Be interested in them; don't try to be interesting

Make them feel valuable

Guide them to exhale—provide space and place (including venting, whining and complaining and ask for more)

Remove the dissonance (when you think you are coming across as one way but people see you in totally different way) and then distrust can dissolve

Share your vulnerabilities

Don't waste your time on toxic people, but when they are unavoidable— make eye contact, act polite, but bored, stand up straight, arms by the side, not in fists, be relaxed

§

"I don't negotiate with terrorists." If I had a hundred bucks for every time I've heard this in a mediation, I would be the proud owner of . . . well, something really expensive.

For context, I serve as a mediator in divorce cases about 2 or 3 times a month and have done so for over 12 years. I've been a divorce lawyer representing people in litigation for more than 20 years now.

Early on in my career, I thought using the word "terrorist" in a divorce situation was extreme and harsh. Frankly, it felt like the person saying it was hypersensitive and was exaggerating. No violence was being threatened. There was no political agenda on behalf of either party.

Then the more I participated in negotiations, the more I read about negotiations and the more I observed negotiations, the more I began to see a connection.

In the strictest sense, there is rarely a terrorist involved in a divorce process, but that doesn't mean that it doesn't feel like you are being intimidated for the gain of the other party during the negotiations.

And when you are operating from a place of fear, LOOK OUT. That subconscious part of your mind will lie, cheat and steal to protect you from the perceived threat.

Goodbye rational, logical, primate brain. Hello reptile brain and its instincts to fight, flee or freeze.

When the reptile brain has taken over, you might as well forget about negotiating with logic UNLESS you can bring someone from reptile brain back to primate brain.

The ability to do that is the best skill of the lawyers and mediators I have observed in negotiations. It can be learned.

Then applied to every form of a negotiation, including ones with your coworkers, your spouse, your friends, your children, your boss, your clients, your sales prospects and more.

BUT . . . these techniques may be unlikely to work with bullies and assholes. First, you need to understand the basics of the reptile brain. It is impulsive. It is in charge of keeping you safe, making it territorial and aggressive. It is reactionary. It is obsessive. It is compulsive. It visualizes and doesn't think in words.

When it is in overdrive, it shuts down all of the rational and thinking parts of our minds.

This reaction is called the Amygdala Hijack.

A very small area deep in your brain senses a threat and flies into action by directing impulses to the frontal cortex (the logical part of your brain) and diverting impulses away from the frontal cortex.

Once the Amygdala has taken over, the ability to reason drops, working memory fails, and stress hormones rage. Interesting, isn't it, how the word "hijack" comes up in the literature? Terrorists. Hijackers. I began to see a pattern.

I looked to books and articles on terrorist negotiations to understand how the FBI and other agencies do what they do.

After reading those materials, the second thing I highly recommend is learning a lot about mirror neurons. On occasion, I have seen these referred to as empathy neurons. For instance, when you are watching a race and your heart starts beating faster as the runners get closer to the finish line, those are mirror neurons at work.

Or when you see someone smile at you and you smile and you begin feeling all the positive feelings that come with a smile.

The research is amazing and continuing to get more advanced in this area. Originally, it focused on mirroring physical acts and how the same neurons were firing in the original actor's brain as the imitator's brain.

Advanced studies are being done now on how we can "read" someone's mind or be "in tune" with them by mirroring their emotions.

Okay, I digress. We don't have to know precisely on a scientific level HOW it works. We only need to know that it does work.

Breathing, deeply breathing and being silent is one of my favorite techniques. Try it sometime in a difficult situation. Stop arguing. Start slowly breathing with deep breaths. It may feel weird or hokey or out of character, but do it.

See if the others in the room begin to mirror you. And then listen. Don't react or respond. Others in the room will begin to fill the silence with questions like what do we do now or what do you think?

Be careful not to give them answers as a key to moving people from reptile brain to primate brain is to get them thinking again.

Instead ask questions. Don't judge their answers. Instead make them feel "felt."

I find that people who are resisting cannot listen until they feel "felt."

Often, the people I encounter in divorce cases feel vulnerable. They are afraid of the changes coming to their lives. They are scared for their financial future. They are worried about their children. I share my vulnerabilities with them, and I ask them to do the same.

The best mediators I have observed do their best to listen without forming conclusions or forming perceptions (or at least they keep those thoughts to themselves).

Never underestimate the power of empathy and placing yourself in someone else's shoes.

Word of caution. You will crash and burn at this if you do not have your own emotions in check first. People can say nasty, hurtful things when their subconscious is going all out to keep them safe.

Never take things personally. In the words of Don Miguel Ruiz, "Whatever happens around you, don't take it personally... Nothing other people do is because of you. It is because of themselves," *The Four Agreements: A Practical Guide to Personal Freedom.*

Once you have someone listening, how do you get them to consider something and then be willing to do it?

Here are some techniques I have used and I have seen others use in negotiations which are very effective:

1. Expect "no" as an answer. Instead of letting it stop there, don't ask what would make you say "yes." Ask what question or concern you failed to address which would have resulted in a different answer. Listen and then respond to what they say. It is a subtle, but a distinct difference.

2. Ask them what would improve their situation. When they say it is impossible, respond with, "Let's first see what would improve your situation and then let's talk about what would need to happen to make it possible."

3. Ask them to "tell you more about that" when they are describing a possible solution.

4. Ask them to role play with you about what they think the other person is thinking and feeling. Explore why they think that is how the other person thinks and feels.

5. Change where you are sitting in the room. It continues to surprise me how much more effective I am negotiating with some people when I move to sit right beside a person instead of across from them. Sometimes I stand up so that their eyes follow me around the room and they stop being fixated on a spot on the floor.

6. We all know that open-ended questions and fill-in-the-blank statements get people thinking more than yes or no ones, but when you are in a difficult negotiation, starting with a series of "yes" questions and then moving to more open-ended ones can lead to traction and then a buy in.

As you go forth, remember, as a coping mechanism, the subconscious often protects us by throwing up terror barriers to make us retreat to places that are known, safe and familiar. Change your approach and you will find that you can overcome the hijack.

7. Family Law

Why do people end up seeing me? For every reason you and every screen and television writer in Hollywood can think of and more.

A million reasons to seek a divorce from infidelity to abuse to boredom to leaving the toilet seat up. Look a little deeper, though, or talk to enough clients, and some bigger truths underlie the reasons.

§

I saw Hamilton on Broadway – it was everything we expected and more. Just a fantastic experience, sign me up for when the traveling show hits North Carolina.

Does this happen to you? After I see a movie, show, TV series, etc., about something or someone historical, I like to look it up and see how much of what I just watched was true. Even though I had read parts of Ron Chernow's *Hamilton*, I was curious about a couple things. So, I looked and while I was doing so it really hit me that finances were the bane of Alexander Hamilton's life.

The irony, of course, is delicious the guy who designed the monetary system and early economy of the United States wallowed in debt and seems to have had a hard time balancing his checkbook. At the very least, it's an interesting juxtaposition.

It's startlingly clear to me that Alexander and Eliza Hamilton would certainly have been divorced if they were around anytime over the last sixty years or so. Divorce was simply not an option for them in the 1790s. The reason for their split wouldn't have been Alexander's affair with Marie Reynolds − Eliza seemed to have genuinely forgiven him − but money.

Money issues (in all their forms), you probably know, is one of the leading reasons for divorce. The Hamiltons had them in spades. Alexander Hamilton grew up in great poverty, Eliza's family was one of the richest in New York. So, the potential for problems was there from the beginning. Alexander was morally (and probably politically) opposed to accepting financial help from Eliza's father, Philip Schuyler.

Alexander was important and had to live that way − nice house, horses, carriage, travel, dining, the works. Eliza was expected to entertain. Lavishly. Alexander was hardly making money as Secretary of the Treasury, yet he was expected to act and live like a gentleman. Gentlemen in the 1790s did not overtly work. Not even in professions like the law and medicine.

Alexander needed to live as a gentleman. At the very least, his position demanded it. Credit was his only avenue to maintain his 'gentleman' status. The Hamiltons were in chronic debt through the 1790s, right up to the duel.

It should be noted, Alexander's affair with Maria Reynolds plunged Hamilton deeper into debt. Reynolds' husband, James, cemented himself as one of the great cads of early American history by blackmailing Alexander. He started with an initial

$1,000 (about $14,000 in today's currency) and smaller amounts – $30, $40 – thereafter. Add that to the stress on his marriage and, well . . .

. . . I have to wonder what the Hamiltons would have done around 1793-94 had divorce been an option. Then I wonder if they would have worked it out in mediation. What those sessions would have been like? Bet if I represented Alexander, Eliza would have shown up with, you guessed it, Aaron Burr.

§

I get this more than every once in a while during consultations, "I know a dozen people who have shared every detail of their divorces with me; I'm great with Google; I'm smart, reasonable, and good with people and numbers; my spouse and I are on the same page . . . so, why should I waste money on an attorney?"

I get all that. I really do. I empathize. My clients are smart – whip smart. They get numbers and most are excellent negotiators in daily life. A few could close any sale, anytime. Others have the uncanny ability to look at problems in unique ways and then solve them. A few are lawyers, a couple are doctors, most are professionals.

My clients have one thing in common, though, they know that smart, successful men and women can screw up their divorces. As do I. I have seen it time after time. Courthouses are rife with stories of people who self-destructed in ways seldom seen anywhere aside, perhaps, politicians.

A great goal in life is to never be the subject of a courthouse story. So, because you're thinking it right now, here's how you can sabotage your divorce. Think of them as 'D'Oh' moments made by people a lot smarter than Homer Simpson.

The 'Mickey Rourke Theorem'. Body Heat, 1982, Mickey Rourke is William Hurt's friend and client. As he watches his buddy about to make a life altering decision, Rourke says (I'm paraphrasing): "Any time you try a decent crime, you got fifty ways you're gonna screw up. If you think of twenty-five of them, then you're a genius... and you ain't no genius." Simply, The Mickey Rourke Theorem applies to all law related matters.

I have a friend who was doing some high-end estate and separation planning in New York back in the 1990's. He worked for months to come up with a fair and equitable plan. Both sides had been very cooperative. The husband asked if my friend could come by his apartment on Fifth Avenue to go over the final documents.

The first thing my friend noticed on his first visit ever to the apartment was a Matisse hanging over the sofa. Completely taken aback, my friend asked a variation on 'What the hell is that doing there?" the response was, "Oh, I forgot about that, is it a problem?"

The short answer – yes. Failure to disclose all the assets may result in a resolution being set aside which can result in the whole division of property being re-negotiated or re-litigated. None of that is a good thing. Both of them are expensive to repair.

Presenting evidence in court, in front of a judge, is not quite the same as the way they do it on *Law & Order, Boston Legal, The Practice,* or the million other 'courtroom dramas' out there. Do you know why they're not the same? Because the real thing is far too boring to build a drama around. There are books about the rules and books about the rules for the rules.

The books – not one of them a bestseller for obvious reasons – written on the rules of evidence would build a pretty tall skyscraper. If you wandered onto an NFL field in the middle of a game and inquired of the guy lining up opposite you what the rules were, he would flatten you before you finished the sentence.

The difference with court is that the harm is to the psyche but lasts much, much, longer. You may know the truth. You may be able to handle the truth. But, if you can't follow the rules and get the evidence in front of the Judge, the Judge will never know the truth.

Yogi Berra said, "I never said most of the things I said." When you are representing yourself and your ex-to-be tosses out something to the court that you know you never said . . . well, you're really not the best person to be trying to deny or defend it. Because you're you. Lawyers are referred to as advocates for a reason.

There are a lot of people who can hit the hell out of a baseball in a batting cage. There's even more who can bash away off a hitting tee. There are about 500 people on the planet who can hit live pitching well enough to play in the MLB. Performing – make no mistake, going to court involves performing – in front of a judge, lawyers, clerks, a courtroom full of mostly strangers is hard. It gets incrementally harder when the audience includes the spouse you are proceeding against.

Courts have rules. Courts have a rather different approach to the rules than the pirates. In court – any court – it's not, ever, "well, it'd be more of a guideline than a rule." You could probably get away with talking like a pirate in court . . . you cannot get away with not following the rules. Those rules are not simple. Wait, scratch that, they sometimes are on the face of it. The rules of chess fit on a single sheet of paper. After four moves there are about 300 billion different combinations of possible moves.

One of most famous, sensational custody cases of the 1930's – covered worldwide – involved the actress Mary Astor. The entire case, and the reason for the sensational media coverage, revolved around her diary. Her ex-husband found it, used the entries (she was a very good writer) against her. The thing here is probably obvious – it's really easy to hide a diary, presumably most people can do it just a little bit better than Mary Astor. It's not at all possible to hide social media.

Try denying/defending something when Twitter/Facebook and the rest show you said it. Or worse.

By the way, Snapchat is not immune, there's this thing called 'screenshots'.

You are under a microscope when going through a divorce. You may be followed by a PI. Your conversations may be recorded. All your texts and emails to your spouse are evidence. All your social media posts can be reviewed by a judge. One brilliant "selfhelper" thought it would be a good idea to post about taking target practice on a photo of his wife. Having a bad day? Maybe. Being sarcastic? Maybe. Maybe not. The damage done when his 8-year old son and Facebook friend saw the post was too much for the Judge to look past. Only an impartial person can point out the utter folly of these things. None of us, really, is capable of managing ourselves when it comes to ... well, ourselves. A divorce proceeding is the one place, the one time, where feelings of paranoia may well be justified.

Thomas Pynchon wrote, "If they can get you asking the wrong questions, they don't have to worry about answers." This is never more true than appearing in court opposite a skilled attorney. That attorney can and will get you to ask the wrong questions and lock you into a never-ending loop. You will never get to the answers you want to get to. Because, rules.

§

This piece was written with my colleague and friend Attorney Sarah Poriss in Hartford, Connecticut.

One of the first things every family law client asks ... what are the odds of [fill in the issue(s) here] happening in my favor?

In a perfect world, any half-way serious review of fast food burgers from around the country would rank the A&W Third-Pound burger right up there with In N' Out and Shake Shack. By all reports the Third-Pound was a burger among burgers. Fresh, grilled, delicious, and it was priced below McDonald's latest, and biggest seller, the ubiquitous Quarter Pounder (or, as Vincent Vega would say, the 'Royale with cheese').

We'd go for one now, it sounds that good. Except we can't — and that has nothing to do with the fact there are a whole lot fewer A&W's around these days than in the early '80's.

It has everything to do with the fact the Third-Pound was a miserable failure. Sure, it was big, sure it was fresh and delicious, sure it was cheaper than a Quarter Pounder. None of that mattered, what mattered was some 40% of the hamburger eating public believed that the Third-Pounder was smaller than the Quarter Pounder. Because 4 is greater than 3.

This happened in the mid-Eighties. It's hardly a stretch to say that America's grasp of mathematics has not improved since the A&W fiasco.

That's a problem.

We are both lawyers, albeit with very different focuses. We both need math – we deal with a variety of financial issues, sometimes complex. But we deal with it. Even though we have the Dr. McCoy excuse – "Dammit, Jim, I'm a lawyer not a mathematician."

While true, when confronted with a knotty financial issue that pops up during a foreclosure or compiling a divorcing couple's assets, we do the math. It's never as hard as it seems before we start.

Getting clients to do the math, though is sometimes daunting. We need forms filled out and basic calculations made before we can do much. But, it's math, and the forms look imposing, and it's personal and in many ways it represents a finality – of a marriage, of a home. So, no one's rushing to get it done.

That's all fine and, somewhat, to be expected. We cajole and remind and bug and get it done.

Our 'Third-Pound' scenario, though, pops up when we're asked 'what are the odds'. "What are the odds I keep the house?" "If I take it to court, what are the odds …?" and every possible variation and scenario.

We've been practicing long enough and intensively enough in our respective areas of concentration to be able to answer this and be pretty damn close. If we answered. But, we are loathe to do so. Because if it's true that the average American is not good with math, then it's even more true that they are really bad with odds.

Not sure about this? Well, poll your friends after the local weather guy predicts a 70% chance of rain and nothing beside a few black clouds roll overhead. You'll find that a more than a few will complain about the 'blown' forecast. In any group of friends and acquaintances, by the way, there is always at least one person who will say, "Ha! They always get the forecast wrong!"

The weatherperson didn't get it wrong, of course. Because there was a 30% chance of it not raining. Not insignificant. Yet most people never heard 70%, they heard 'It will rain.' Because 70 is closer to 100 than 30 is.

As most legal matters are just a little bit more important than a rain shower, you could see where giving odds could be problematic.

Then, there's the flip side of this. The Patriots won a Super Bowl after being down 25 points in the third quarter. At the time, the odds (they were calculated online as the game went on by various sites) gave them a .4% chance of winning. When they were down 28-20 with four minutes left, they had an 8% chance of winning.

But they won. Coming back from a deficit like that hadn't happened in 50 previous Super Bowls. Statistics tell us it shouldn't happen again for at least another 50. Though statistics

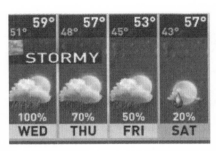

also tell us it could happen again next year, then not repeat for another 100 or more Super Bowls.

Rare is rare, but there's no telling when it might pop up.

Which leads to another math problem for lawyers. Instead of the Third-Pound Dilemma, it's the 'So you're telling me there's a chance dilemma', as in the great bit in *Dumb and Dumber*:

> Lloyd Christmas: What are the chances of a guy like you and a girl like me... ending up together?
>
> Mary Swanson: Not good.
>
> Lloyd Christmas: Not good like one in a hundred?

Mary Swanson: I'd say more like one in a million.

Lloyd Christmas: So, you're telling me there's a chance?

Put these two dilemmas together and we think you'll understand why we are really, really careful answering 'what are the odds' questions.

§

Filing for divorce, or bringing any family law matter forward, come to think of it, requires getting through some barriers – personally – first.

One is taking on adversity.

Take Opening Day. Real spring finally arrives with the first real baseball games. It makes things ... right somehow. Seven months now of nightly baseball, the absolutely best thing to have on in the background while getting work done. The only sport conducive to increasing productivity during the season.

This is a baseball story. I don't think it's debatable that, as Ted Williams said, that baseball is mentally tougher than any other sport. One hundred and sixty-two regular season games, 500-600 chances a year to fail at the plate, 200 innings or more to get tattooed, 50-60 relief appearances a year to walk to the mound in front of 40,000 people, throw two or three pitches and blow the game.

Baseball is awash in pitfalls. Very visible pitfalls. Ted Williams was probably the greatest overall hitter to ever live (before you object, please look at his numbers, then recall that he lost five prime seasons flying fighters for the Marines). His lifetime batting average is .344. That means that for every thousand times at bat, he made 656 outs.

Good players handle the bad, great players smack it away.

I heard this story years ago, it has stuck with me for years for, I think, a lot of reasons.

In 1975 the (woeful) San Diego Padres traded one of their few stars, Nate Colbert, to the Detroit Tigers. Nate was a hulking first baseman who hit a lot of home runs in a very unfriendly home run park while sporting McDonald's colors.

He did not get off to a great start, but he was usually a slow starter and no one was too concerned. Still, it's always tough to go into a batting slump, even the best hitters have to fight back the nagging feeling 'this is it, I'm done,' after going 1 for 30.

Fourteen games into the young season the Tigers played the Red Sox. Luis Tiant started, finished, gave up one unearned run and lost 1-0. Colbert went hitless with a strikeout. After the game he went into such a tailspin that a month later he was released, went back to the National League and the Montreal Expos (yes, there was a team in Montreal) and was out of baseball a year later at the tender age of 30. A three-time National League All-Star, gone.

The story I read, somewhere in the foggy past, was that Colbert told *Sports Illustrated* that Tiant ended his career. He wasn't beaned. He wasn't intimidated. He was, however, so utterly baffled, confused, and dazzled he never recovered his batting eye.

Odds are you have no idea who Luis Tiant is, despite the fact he won 229 major league games, was a renown big-game pitcher, and pitched until he was 41.

That describes exactly nothing when it comes to El Tiante. He was a whirl of motion when he pitched. He turned his back on the batter – completely. He looked up at the heavens instead of the general direction of the plate. Fernando Venezuela copied him and Ebby Calvin 'Nuke' LaLoosh in Bull Durham copied Fernando. Tiant was very much the original.

Tiant threw every pitch known to man, all at different speeds and arm angles. No one knew what was coming or where it was headed … remember, he never looked at the hitter. Batting against Tiant was an adventure, it was unnerving, discombobulating.

Colbert had never seen him, never mind hit against him. Tiant may have destroyed his timing but he certainly destroyed his confidence at a particularly vulnerable time. Nate was facing enough adversity; Luis finished him off, however inadvertently.

Here's the thing, though, about Luis Tiant: he had overcome adversity, soul-crushing adversity, more than once before he became a celebrated – to this day – Boston icon. The son of a legendary left-handed pitcher for the equally legendary New York Cubans of the Negro league, Tiant defected from Castro's Cuba in 1961. He did not see his parents for 18 years.

He was signed by the Cleveland Indians, endured racism playing in the minors in Charleston, SC, exacerbated by the fact he was still learning English. Despite this, called up to the Indians in 1964 his first start was against the first place (of course) Yankees in Yankee Stadium. He won, a complete game 3-0 shutout, four hits (all singles), 11 strikeouts, beating Whitey Ford.

By the end of the 1968 season he was a star, he won 21 games, led the league in ERA at a ridiculously low 1.69. He set a slew of single season records. He was 28, almost exactly the same age Colbert was when he faced him for the first time, and the sky was the limit.

It fell apart quickly. Like Colbert, when Luis was 30 he was out of baseball. Arm and confidence problems fed on each other and he was a shadow of the player who strolled into Yankee

Stadium and shut down the American League Champions. He was released in spring training 1971.

The Atlanta Braves took a flyer on the former 20 game winner and signed him to a minor league contract in May. He pitched well enough for the historically pitching-poor Red Sox to pick him up and assign him to their AAA team. He made it back to the majors with Boston in 1971 and he was awful.

Consigned to the bullpen at the start of 1972, at age 31, he pitched in relief in lost causes early in the season. But, he looked better. An injury here, an injury there, and he was a starter by June. He won 15 games and the American League ERA title. He went on to become that Boston icon and serious Hall of Fame contender.

Nate and Luis, different adversity, different responses.

I think our responses to adversity can define us over time.

I am very aware that every one of my clients is facing adversity. My hope is to help guide them toward the Luis Tiant response.

§

I don't normally do this but, here goes, it is indisputable that *Planes, Trains, and Automobiles* is the greatest movie ever made about Thanksgiving. I usually invite discussion, even dissension, but not here. It is, subject closed.

Planes, Trains, and Automobiles is funny as hell, even on its hundredth or so viewing. It's also affecting. Great dialog, great characters, even in the age of cell phones and Venmo and a dozen different ways to transfer information and cash instantaneously, it still works. Because ... people. (ok, that and the fact that travel by planes and bus and train hasn't exactly improved a lot since 1988).

There's another dimension to it, though, it hit me a little while back, before I was really blogging. It's this – the relationship between Del Griffith and Neal Page is a backward study of the kind of relationship I deal with every day.

Del (the late, great John Candy) and Neal (Steve Martin) are thrown together by chance, but they certainly don't meet cute. Their relationship starts out like many – many– relationships end. Every little thing Del does gets under Neal's skin, every raised eyebrow and nasty look and passive-aggressive remark that Neal makes gets to Del, though he doesn't show it.

But, of course, they go through a series of life-altering events, being robbed, having a train engine explode, taking a ride on a jammed bus (great line: Del, "Have you ever taken a bus trip before?" "No." "Well, it's not going to improve your mood"), a rental car disaster, more.

They get through the travails of traveling during the Thanksgiving rush. By the end, they've reached an emotional understanding, the kind of connection most relationships start out with. They would never had reached this point if not for the circumstances that keep them together – the only reasons they would ever stay together after their first few meetings . . . they are that different.

It really is a reverse microcosm of relationships. I think if clients can remember the connection and when they got through tough times like burning up the rental car while forgetting the dirty socks in the sink they can get to the next phase of their lives in great shape.

And that's the goal. Right?

8. Meditations on Mediation

HBO's [hideous] show, *Divorce*, had at least three characters over several episodes in its first season describe mediation as the process by which, "one person gets the coffee and the other one gets the cup."

That's patently ridiculous but try telling that to 20-30 million or so viewers, I mean, Sarah Jessica Parker wouldn't lie to them, right?

Well, she did, here's what mediation really is.

§

A very different kind of Sci-fi movie came out in the late Fall – *Arrival*. Sure, there were aliens – fairly odd ones at that – the usual military involvement, enormous spacecraft setting up at 12 sites around the world at once, the threat of all-out war hanging over everything, and . . .

. . . well, that's just the thing. The 'and' here are a linguist, a team of computer experts, and a theoretical physicist working hand-in-hand to figure out what the aliens want. That's it. No *Independence Day* pyrotechnics here, just a lot of talking and theory and intelligence.

What's striking about *Arrival* is that it's all about communication – which is why I'm writing about it. Actually, I'm writing about it because *Arrival* is also about *learning* to communicate. Starting from scratch.

It all revolves around the absolute need to not bring any preconceived notions or assumptions to the table. None. Intent is as important as it is hard to ascertain. At an early point in the movie, the linguist, Dr. Banks (Amy Adams – amazing) explains, "We need them to understand the difference between a weapon and a tool. Language can be messy, and sometimes one can be both." What matters is the intent of the person with the hammer.

What the movie makes startlingly clear is that communication cannot be a 'zero sum game', i.e., it can't be about winning or losing. Dr. Banks' military supervisor, an impatient but supportive Army colonel (Forrest Whitaker), asks her at one point why she doesn't try to teach the aliens chess to facilitate communication. Dr. Banks is appalled. She, very nicely, explains that that would be completely counterproductive. Competition, she says, is repugnant to honest communication.

It's not often I can sit in a movie and be so struck at how sharply it speaks to me and my practice.

Nowhere is the need to win more out of place than in a divorce. Nowhere is the need to communicate more vital than during a divorce. That would be communication with one's lawyer and communication between the parties.

In *Arrival,* Dr. Banks is engaged in a non-zero-sum game with the aliens – a successful outcome will benefit both parties. In non-zero-sum games the players' interests may be different, but they also very much overlap.

I mediate because the alternatives in family law tend to become zero-sum. That's not good, because that means someone is going to lose. Often it is the children.

Don't get me wrong, I love zero-sum games, I watch one along with a few hundred million other people every February. The NFL is welcome to their zero-sum game, I prefer my clients go in the entirely different direction and settle things as intelligently and diplomatically and in mutually beneficial manner as Dr. Banks does.

§

It's fashionable to talk about chess and mediation in the same breath – as in, mediation is a chess match, one side moves, the other side reacts, makes a move based on the changing 'board.' In this metaphor, it helps to think at least a few moves ahead, anticipate the other side, maybe even feint, certainly keep the moves to yourself (and lawyer), and, of course, never blink.

A grand chess match, then, to reach an agreement acceptable to both parties while avoiding having an uninterested third-party make the decision for them. Friends, clients, family have made the analogy, I've used it myself – or at least obliquely

– over the years. It's, admittedly, an easy crutch of an image to impart to clients already feeling the stress of starting an action.

The thing is, though, it's not an apt metaphor. In any way, really. See, I'm not a big chess player. I find the rules just a bit too confining. But, I get the game and see its complexities. I don't play on anything close to a consistent basis and I suspect not all that many people do. Chess is kind of like that deep, intellectual book everyone is raving about and everyone is carrying around to Starbucks and the beach and no one is reading.

Because of this, we are all overlooking a basic but key element of chess: people play to win. Chess is a great intellectual exercise but the minute two people are sitting across from one another make no mistake, it's about winning.

This was really hammered home by last year's *Pawn Sacrifice*, the story of the Bobby Fischer – Boris Spassky chess championship in the early '70s. Toby McGuire did an amazing job portraying Fischer and his mental deterioration. The movie takes the position, clearly, that the stresses of high-level chess played a big part in that deterioration. Winning is everything.

I'm struck by this – it's from the film but it's also directly from Fischer's life: In an interview with a magazine, Fischer's coach explains to an uninitiated reporter, "after the first four moves of any chess game there are 300 billion possible move combinations."

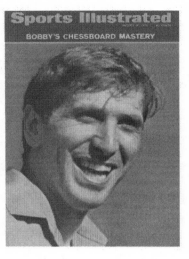

Sure, that's a staggering amount of combinations and, on a lesser scale, it does conjure images of working through a mediation. It's Fischer's response to his coach's assertion that blows the metaphor apart: "People think there are all these options, but there is only one right move."

"Only one right move." It's true for chess. A million, million possible combinations after every move, but only one right one if you want to win. Need to win.

It's not remotely true in mediation. A single individual does not win at mediation. The parties win. They win by putting aside the need to win, not going to war, not searching for the 'right move', and working it out. They do not let a stranger decide for them.

In this regard, the only thing that chess and mediation share is the concept of the sacrifice. But for completely different reasons to completely different ends.

I'll be sure to correct people who use this comparison from here on out, especially clients – I'd hate to give a serious chess player the wrong idea.

§

I get the occasional 'might-be-a-client' who is not really sold on the concept of bringing an attorney into mediation...or negotiations or with the divorce in general.

The thinking is—'I'm a fair guy or gal, perfectly reasonable, we're still friends, LegalZoom and a thousand, thousand Facebook and blog posts show me how to manage this process, so...

That can leave me in the curious and unenviable position of pointing out that no one on the planet is that fair when it comes to something that will affect them on such a personal level, for, like, forever.

By fair, I mean to the ex-spouse-to-be, or the children, or themselves. It would take the wisdom of Solomon—and he was all for cutting the kid in two.

So, in response, I strip the fairness and go to thinking. As in, you hire me to think of the stuff you will never think of. Because all your innate fairness and intensive readings about

North Carolina divorce law and mediation practice may train you to recognize the box, may get you up and running and operating in the box, but will never show you how to think outside it.

To illustrate, let me share a favorite story: In World War II  the US Army established an intelligence section— The Statistical Research Group (SRG)—near Columbia University. Armed with pens, paper, and Marchant desktop calculations, they figured out 'stuff'—like the optimal curve a fighter would take to keep an enemy plane in its gun-sights.

In 1943 the Army Air Corps went to the SRG with what they thought was a pretty straight forward question. It went like this: their bombers now flying into Germany were taking a dreadful pounding. They—mostly B-17s—obviously needed more armor to protect them, more armor means less range, less maneuverability, help us figure out the 'perfect' mix.

The Army had numbers, research performed in the field: when B-17s returned to England they had more bullet holes per square foot on the fuselage than anywhere else.

So SRG spent a great deal of time, effort, and crumpled paper in figuring out how to efficiently armor a B-17s fuselage. The Army's was simple logic: armor goes where the bullet holes are. Obviously.

But, after a lot of calculations were furiously made, a statistical genius named Abraham Wald, blew everyone's collective minds when he announced that the question wasn't 'where are the bullet holes?' it was 'where aren't the bullet holes?'

He noted something everyone—as in everyone—had missed, the Army Air Corps was counting bullet holes in the planes that had returned from combat. There were, then, missing holes'—the holes in the downed planes.

He further noted that the fewest bullet holes per square foot were on the engines. Those were the missing holes—for the same reason there are more people in the hospital with bullet wounds in their legs than bullet wounds in the chest, shots to the engine were usually fatal.

You put the armor where the holes aren't—the engines, the statistics merely proved what was already obvious to everyone who flew in them: B-17s could survive many, many hits to the fuselage.

This wasn't so much 'thinking outside the box' as rethinking the hypothesis he was handed—in other words his client was asking the wrong question.

He knew to ask the right one.

§

Mediation may require working things out, but it also still requires that decisions be made.

I think people sometimes think that going into mediation somehow relieves them of the onus of having to make decisions. That, somehow, the process takes over and shapes and molds the final agreement without the need to make what can be gut-wrenching decisions.

That, of course, is not true, mediation requires decisions across a wide spectrum of issues. Decisions, then, have to be made often. I can't make those decisions for my clients, I can only advise.

Here's a story about decision making:

I have a friend who was a pretty good soccer player into his mid-40's. In the late 80's he was asked to play for a team managed by Tony DiCicco. Tony, you may know, became the coach of the U.S. National Women's Team in the 90's that won two Olympic Golds and the iconic 1999 Women's World Cup. He's now a soccer analyst for ESPN.

At the time, Tony was the Men's National Goalkeeping coach. My friend was a keeper and well aware of Tony's soccer pedigree.

It was, then, somewhat a stressful situation. It didn't get any less stressful over the first weeks of the winter indoor soccer season.

Four games, four shutouts ... and not a word, good, bad, indifferent, from Tony.

A nod before the game, a nod after but not a word.

It was somewhat unnerving for my friend, but a win is a win and a shutout in a premier indoor soccer league is pretty cool.

The fifth game was very different. He gave up a quick goal on a great shot – streak over, fine, the team scored two and all was right with the world.

Late – very late – in the game, the other team ran down the sideline, a midfielder took the ball to the corner, unleashed a vicious cross about twenty feet in front of the goal.

My friend came flying out at it, realized half way there he wasn't going to make it, back peddled, stopped ... and a soccer ball doing about 75 mph whizzed by his head on its way to zipping into the upper left-hand corner of the net.

2-2 tie with the team they shared first place with.

This day, on way to the bar, Tony bolted over to him, put him in a bear hug and said, "Thank God you finally gave up a goal, now I can talk to you."

"Yeah, well, that goal –"

"Forget it, great game," Tony gushed and praised for a minute, then got to it, "so, about that goal –"

"I –"

"Doesn't matter," Tony snapped, "I don't care ... the only thing I care about is this: make a decision – come out, come half way, stay on your line, it's up to you – just make a decision and stick with it.

"You do that and I will always back you up, no one will ever second-guess you. Never ... never don't *not* make a decision again – then we'll have a serious talk."

It was a bit (lot) more profane than that but it stuck with my friend and he tells this story whenever there's a situation that calls for decisions and people do anything but make them.

In other words, he tells this story a lot, because a lot of people are, for a lot of reasons, loathe to pull the trigger on a decision.

I said earlier that I can't make a decision for a client. I can and am, however, more than able to be Tony – I'm here for my clients and will support their well-reasoned decisions. As long as they get made.

§

So ... I watch a lot of college basketball. Live and on TV. A *lot* of basketball. Along with a good chunk of most of the people I know. Three weeks of win and move on, lose and go home. That's it. Sixty-seven of the sixty-eight teams invited to this tournament will have exactly the same experience when a final whistle blows. They lose and go back to their campus.

Maryland was blown out by Xavier, SMU lost at the buzzer

to UCLA, Providence blew a
17-point lead late in the
second half and lost to USC.
Maryland, SMU, and
Providence are at home
watching the games the same
as the rest of us, it's lose, go
home, no style points.

A friend of mine, a
lawyer of sorts (it's
complicated) was talking to a
lawyer friend last week about
a client he had run across. The woman had received a three-page
letter from her attorney telling her where her lawsuit - a business
matter – stood and she needed a 'translation.' My friend shared
it with his lawyer friend because ... well, here: "For two and
three-quarter pages," my friend explained, "the law firm's letter
reiterated how strong her case was, how much the judge 'got' her
points; how much he empathized. The judge's written decision
showed he was on her side in all of it, really didn't like the
defendant and her lawyers. He clearly wanted to not only find
for her, but to really punish the defendant."

"And the last quarter of the letter?" His lawyer buddy asked.

"You lost, you played great, and the judge wishes you won."

His friend thought for a second, then, "That's like telling Princeton — hey, you lost at the buzzer to Notre Dame but, you know what? We're going to fly you to the next round so you can watch the teams that went through."

Again, no style points.

Win and move on, lose and go home is suspenseful and riveting and should be confined to sports and very few other human endeavors. It certainly shouldn't be anywhere near a family law matter. With children, with your life, it isn't worth feeling like the other 67 teams will feel a week from tomorrow night. It's not even worth taking the chance.

I do as much mediation as possible because it's not about winning or losing or even playing a game, it's about working toward a new life.

9. Clients are People Too

Let's face it; we all have jerks in our lives. Family members, spouses, friends, co-workers, bosses, you name it. Now of course I don't mean your family, friends or co-workers . . . or do I?

Everyone has a bad day, so I am not talking about temporary jerks or situational jerks. I'm talking about the real jerks, the people with no self-awareness and only enough emotional intelligence to use it to poke, prod or get what they want purely for their benefit and entertainment.

Ring any bells?

Here are some more signs you might notice; these are people who:

- No Room for Gray. See things only in black and white with nuance shades of gray.
- Power Out Personality. People with really intense behavior, like yelling, impulsive.
- Drama Kings and Queens. Everything amplified, overdone.

- Finger Pointers. Blaming others and not taking responsibility for their own actions.

Emotional responses are over the top with jerks. Let me lead with a little advice from twenty years of family law and mediation practice, and some personal experience. If you can't "beat" them, please don't join them. *PLEASE!*

If you attack them; they attack you. A never-ending circle of attacks. If you want them out of your life, be careful how you do it because true high-conflict people will ramp up the "crazy" and dig in deeper if you cut all ties immediately, rather than slowly moving on.

Disclaimer. I am not a psychologist. I have a Bachelor of Science in psychology in which I learned a little about personality disorders, but please understand I am in no way qualified to make any diagnosis about your friends, spouse, family members, etc.

However, I am in the business of keeping nice people from getting messed up and over in their divorce. Sometimes those people are or become jerks and my job focuses on saving them from themselves, their *jerkhood* status, temporary or permanent.

In the 20 years I have served as a divorce lawyer and 12 years as a mediator, I've developed a working theory about why some divorces cost tons more than others.

Most of the divorces I have handled where the legal fees (for both sides) exceeded $100,000 have a common thread– a spouse with a high-conflict personality while the other spouse doesn't know how to avoid the eggshells and landmines.

How do we stop this madness and how have I maneuvered through the tangled web of divorce disagreements and acrimony? How do you, pre-divorce, maybe thinking about it but not pulling the trigger quite yet, protect yourself from the barrage of blame, negativity and character assassination while trying to have a life, work, raise kids? How do you cope with a person who intensely blames others and cannot seem to stop?

Most of what I've learned and tested in my practice, I've learned from hard-earned experience and my peers and colleagues – even from my supposed adversaries. (Let me also give a shout out to seminars and books by people like Bill Eddy, one of the gurus of dealing with high-conflict people).

The first thing I learned was that you have to change your mindset. Before responding to someone's negative words, you must – first – think about whether your response will trigger a defensive response. If so, don't say it! Can you engage with them and not trigger defensiveness? Yes, but it takes a lot of hard work and retraining your response system.

Consider whether you need to respond at all. And if you do believe that a response is required, avoid common responses which your subconscious shoots directly to your mouth before your conscious self can intervene. You know what they are, you say them every time you are under attack: admonishments, advice, apologies. The Triple A's.

Try training yourself to instead respond with what Bill Eddy calls BIFF statements—Brief, Informative, Friendly and Firm.

If you are sending your response in writing, please have someone else read it as others often see things we don't. Did you know that after Lincoln died his secretaries found dozens of letters in his desk written in the heat of the moment then shelved for being too harsh and counterproductive?

Wait. And wait some more. More than occasionally, I read my clients' responses with them and help decide whether it is a BIFF response or not. BIFF responses aren't nearly as much fun or cathartic as knee jerk reactions, but that's the point. Stop the cycle. Instead of keeping score of zingers and insults, clients are now noticing how much more relief they feel and how quickly the high-conflict situation is defused.

So, about the clients I work with through all this . . .

§

Who won't I take as a client?

I'm wrote this while iced in. Ok, not just me but a pretty good chunk of the greater Raleigh area. This is not normal, this is North Carolina, we are ... coping.

I've just discovered what people in Vermont, Montana, and all of Canada have known since birth – snow and ice in the right quantities/mix lead to some pretty wild thinking after a day or so.

So, I started thinking about clients. Clients, past and present certainly, but mostly future clients. Specifically, probably around the 36th hour of flipping through the Netflix rotation (including the 'Watch it Again' section), *who wouldn't I want as a client?*

That's a question that every attorney should ask herself, but it's a tough concept to address in the non-ice-bound world. Because it sounds mean. It sounds like I'm excluding. It sounds ... pompous ... out of context. Like, 'I would never represent a father who ..."; "I would never represent a mom who ..."; and on and on.

It's none of that. My 'client I wouldn't represent if they offered vast riches; the real location of Atlantis; the secret JFK assassination files; and Elvis' whereabouts isn't a who or a what, it's a way of thinking.

This is best summed up by a wonderful story Bill James relates in his Baseball Abstract (I'm pretty sure it's in every edition). In 1916 Ty Cobb was the best hitter in baseball and probably the most famous man in America. Going into the 1916 season he had won nine consecutive batting titles averaging .376 per season.

That's about the time that Detroit Tigers manager Hughie Jennings received a telegram from an 18-year old kid out in the boondocks of Michigan. It was short and to the point – he could strike out Cobb on three pitches. If Hughie would send him $1.80 for train fare he'd zip down to Detroit and prove it.

For $1.80, Hughie had to know, so he sent it and the kid – very tall, very gangling – showed up. Presumably after a decent warm up, which Cobb presumably watched, the kid got to pitch to the guy who was about to have his first off-year with a .371 average.

It went ... poorly. As James related: *"Cobb hit his first pitch against the right field wall. His second pitch went over the right field wall. The third pitch went over the center field wall. Cobb was thinking they ought to keep this guy around to help him get into a groove."*

It should be noted, by the way, that at the time the center field wall in Nevin Field (later Briggs and Tiger Stadium) was 467 feet away.

The carnage over, Jennings went out to the mound and asked the kid what he had to say for himself.

The kid looked into the batter's box and replied, *"I don't believe that's Ty Cobb in there."*

There's a lot to take from that. This is where I'm at – I want the client who's willing to take on the Ty Cobbs of the world. I emphatically don't want the clients who don't accept reality.

§

And ....

Back in the '80s Newsweek launched a magazine, *Inside Sports*. It was a great magazine. It came out monthly and had articles from great writers, award winning writers, writers that were sports fans but not necessarily sports writers. A sport magazine with some literary aspirations.

It folded after about ten years, which was sad but not unexpected – *Inside Sports* almost perfectly mirrored the rise of ESPN from Canadian Football and Australian Rules Football reruns to dominating the sports scene.

I'm relaying this bit of trivia as a way of explaining that what I'm about to write can't be backed up by any quotes or references. *Inside Sports* blinked out of existence before the

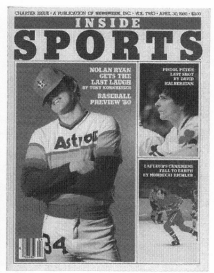

Internet took over and things got digitized and archived forever. I can find some of the old *Inside Sports* covers on-line, but not an article lives on. And, that's a shame because the piece I'm thinking about was brilliant, the kind that back in the day before something could be shared a hundred different ways in a nano-second was handed around groups of friends until it fell apart.

So, the article: it was about a boxer in the 1950s who just wanted one shot at taking on Rocky Marciano for the heavyweight title. This was a guy who traveled the country fighting wherever, whenever he could. Theaters, high school gyms, the occasional decent sized arena, maybe a rare Friday Night Fights TV appearance. His middle name could have been Undercard.

He was the guy, for a while, who up and coming contenders fought to move on. You know, "get by the Killer Swede and you'll get at shot at the tenth ranked contender."

I say 'for while' because it didn't take long for the word to get out that while he was slow and clumsy, he was virtually impossible to knock-out. He could and would take as much punishment as anyone could mete out over 12 rounds or more. And still be standing.

There wasn't much question a good, rising boxer would beat him on his way up the ladder. But fighting him was exhausting. He never went down and he never backed off. Bashing him around to rack up points, then dancing away for the rest of the night was not an option, because this guy never went away.

So, thus far you're probably thinking this a bit about the virtues of 'never giving up', fighting it out to the end, and yada, yada, yada.

It's not. If I was going to do that, I would just recap the last game I watched.

Here's the thing about our hero (I'm sure he had a great name, I don't remember) – he kept boxing because he thought he was good. Strike that, he knew he was good. Despite the losses, despite the scarring, despite his blood-soaked trunks, he was sure he was close to greatness. Every night.

He was as impervious to his mediocrity as he was to getting punched. As a matter of fact, being hit didn't bother him one bit. He was convinced if he just took a few more hits from a few more higher ranked fighters he would rise through the ranks  himself. I suppose he thought he'd be the Bizzaro World Heavyweight Champion.

Our guy had one goal in life, he wanted to fight Rocky Marciano. Marciano, in the 1950s, was as big a name as there was in sports. He was the champ and he was well on his way to a 49-0 record with 43 knockouts.

It was news of national import when Marciano *didn't* knock an opponent out. Yet our guy, a human punching bag, begged and cajoled his manager for years to set up a fight with the Champ.

His manager, surely a patient soul, wouldn't allow it. The punchline of the piece came toward the end, when our hero says, "Look, what are you worried about? Do you think if my grandmother punched me on one cheek and Marciano punched me on the other, I could tell the difference?"

His manager thought for a moment and replied, "No, and that's precisely the problem."

Nothing much scares me in my practice. Except this. I never saw this guy box, but sure have run across the type – men and women – more often than I'd have liked. They are the client that fights for fighting's sake, or over little things because in their mind everything is important. And they are impervious to nuance and loss.

I won't represent this type of client (life is too short) but I do represent their spouses. When I run into them on the other side, I resent the fact that they force me to be Marciano with them. Though, I suppose, I shouldn't worry, they don't notice anyway.

§

And ...

It took a cartoon – albeit, a funny, wicked, insane cartoon – on Adult Swim to bring home the type of client I don't quite get. It's a type familiar to most of us. They are separated – in word if not in fact – and definitely going to pull the trigger on a divorce and everything that goes with it ... real soon. The problem is – and may always be – that there's always a reason for not moving forward. On one side it's a feeling of guilt and/or shame and/or abysmally low self-esteem and/or fear. The other? Just flip it around.

This is especially exacerbated where the other person in the relationship is the flip side of one or more of the above. This forms the basis of a codependency and I'm here to tell you that it is a bear to work with in family law.

I have a friend who filed for divorce five years ago. Then withdrew it. Then separated. Is now filing again. And ... we'll see. A former client dragged her separation out for over four years, every time we tried to address an ending (any ending, at that point) guilt and shame reared their ugly heads and we took three steps back from whence we came.

I tend not to dwell on these things, and usually do that pretty well, but when I'm zipping through channels at 11:30 at night and stumble across the awesome Rick and Morty and they are absolutely nailing it in a show about family therapy ... well, I'm blown away.

For those of you who haven't discovered it yet, Rick and Morty is insane, cynical, and brilliant. It's loosely based on *Back to the Future*, with a kid, Morty, zipping around the galaxy with his grandfather, Rick, the smartest man in the galaxy – as he reminds us several times a show.

Their extended family is, to be kind, dysfunctional. Morty's parents have passive-aggressiveness and great one-liners under their breaths down cold. Mid-way through Season Two, Rick's had enough. He orders Jerry and Beth into his space car and takes them to a therapy planet with a 100% success rate repairing marriages.

So, that's the set up. The therapist explains that "the next step is to watch your mythologs interact together. It's never pretty, we need to remember that we are not the monsters we sometimes see each other as because we are real and we are functional, that's what makes us better than them. We find solutions, we can adapt, we can communicate, and most importantly, we can work together."

Great stuff, right? Beth and Jerry seem on the path to fixing everything. Until their mythologs interact and proceed to destroy the planet.

The therapist realizes his mistake too late, screams, "Oh, dear God, no .... they're codependent!"

I can feel the same way when confronted with a client with codependency issues. My best bet, refer the client to a therapist. Rick has this to say about Earth therapy: "You might just as well ask a horse to fix a merry-go-round. I mean, he'll try his best but mostly he's just going to be horrified."

It's a great (deep, too) line but it's not my experience. Therapy can work, and boy do I need it with a client's codependency.

§

We still talk about it today, it was *the* defining moment of the 19th Century. June 18, 1815, the Battle of Waterloo. The 'near-run' battle that saw Napoleon defeated for good and the end of twenty-plus years of almost continuous warfare throughout Europe.

It was a brutal day and the battle wasn't decided until late evening. The Duke of Wellington, a stoic rock on the field, collapsed that night, in tears, shaking with emotion. He tried to sleep on a pallet while a trusted aide was lying on his bed, dying. He didn't write his report on the battle until late into the next day, while the wounded were still being culled off the field.

In the days before telegrams, it was a great honor to be chosen to deliver a victory message back to London.

Wellington's choices were few, many of his aides, his second in command, dozens of generals were dead, dying, or badly wounded.

Wellington finished his report and gave it to Lieutenant Colonel The Honourable Henry Percy, his sole surviving Aide-de-camp.

Percy set off for London, still in the uniform he wore at Waterloo. He reached London at 10 PM on the 21st. He tried to present the dispatch at Downing Street, everybody who was anybody was at a dinner party being thrown by a certain high society hopeful named Mrs. Boehm. It was the social event of the year. Percy jumped back in his carriage and went directly to the Boehm home where he was told he would find His Royal Highness, the Prince Regent, soon to be King George IV.

He rushed into the home carrying two captured French Eagles. No one who was there ever forgot the pure drama of the moment when Percy approached the Prince, knelt, and proclaimed, "Victory, Sir, Victory!"

No one, that is, except for Mrs. Boehm. Her take on the historic moment:

"Very few of His Majesty's subjects ever had a more superb assembly collected together than I had on the night of June 21st, 1815. That dreadful night! Mr. Boehm had spared no cost to render it the most brilliant party of the season, but all to no purpose! Never did a party promising so much, terminate so disastrously! All our trouble, anxiety, and expense were utterly thrown away in consequence of what shall I say? Well, I must say it – the unseasonable declaration of the Waterloo victory. Of course one was very glad to think we had beaten those horrid French; but still, I shall always think it would have been far better if Henry Percy had waited quietly till the morning, instead of bursting in upon us as he did in such indecent haste."

'Such indecent haste." That sums it up. The one type of potential client we really can't abide, the 'yes, but what about me' person. No matter the circumstance – sickness, bad weather, natural disaster, news of the battle that changed European and World history forever – it's all about them.

Not the ideal client in a family law setting.

§

Halt and Catch Fire is the best TV show of the last four years that you probably haven't seen. Critically acclaimed, but on AMC on Saturday nights, nowhere near *The Walking Dead* or *Breaking Bad* reruns. *Halt and Catch Fire* is the story of the beginnings of the age of personal computers and the internet. It's a show where you think you may know what's coming, but it seldom happens the way you think it will. Which is part of its brilliance.

It seems like the internet has been around forever, and God knows what we would do without it, but, of course, that's far from the truth. The internet existed long before we could dial into AOL and grit our teeth through the buzz, static, ringing, and white noise until connected.

The internet has been around since the early '60's. It was primarily for government (especially the Department of Defense) and educational purposes. The first computer hackers discovered the 'net' while the first personal computer entrepreneurs recognized (in some form, they would all be amazed if dropped down from 1985 to today) its potential.

So, a couple of characters in *Halt and Catch Fire* try to get at the net, illegally and through subterfuge. One just hacks his way into the DOD 'site'. He is a brilliant coder, he gets in, does what he needs to do, erases his hard drives, does a few more things, and is pretty pleased with himself that he pulled it off.

He is surprised, then, when the FBI comes to his door, but he handles it with the aplomb of a guy who knows there's not a shred of evidence anywhere. A guy about his age (young) walks to his computer, plugs in a black box, and goes to work.

Our guy wants to know what's going on. The man at the computer explains that a few months ago he was just like him, since the FBI caught him, he hacks for them. Then he explains the black box, simply, with "It will find everything ... because nothing you do can really erase anything. Ever."

That was true at the dawn of the internet (ask the kid from *War Games*) and it's true today. In spades. As President Trump found out when he 'erased' his tweets showing support for the failed candidacy of Luther Strange. There is just no such thing, in the age of screen saves and advanced algorithms, everything posted online is basically eternal.

The only safe assumption to make on social media is that anything you post will always be there. I think most people know this. Every lawyer I know who does any type of litigation whatsoever certainly knows this.

So, here's the thing – if you think you might become involved in a family law matter, if you're in the midst of a family law matter, if you've just finished a family law matter, understand that anything you post on Facebook, Twitter, Snapchat, and almost any other platform you can think of, can be found and can be used by people not disposed to be kind to you.

A woman in California recently had a large emotional pain and suffering award cut in half because the defense found a bunch of Facebook posts where she talked about how happy she was; a father in the Midwest lost shared custody because he liked some posts in favor of marijuana; the list grows longer every day.

Social media is great like a lot of things are great. Like a lot of things that are great, too much or indiscriminate use can lead to real problems. In a perfect world our clients would go off social media while their cases are pending. We recognize this is not a perfect world and our clients want to continue to be connected to the world and their on-line support groups. We just ask that's it done wisely.

§

This is a little complicated, so bear with me for a minute or three. I just ran across a reference to an old PBS show, *Connections*. That set off bells. That show was ... amazing. Hosted by a British Historian named James Burke, it was so indelibly different you couldn't help but to not only be enthralled but to remember the vast chunks of totally unrelated stuff Burke threw at you. At the very least, if you got nothing else out of the show, you were set to win trivia contests for a very, very long time.

Here's how the show worked – Burke, pleasant, funny, charming, and slightly sarcastic – would start with something out of the past – ancient history, medicine, agriculture, germs, science, literature, religion, you name it, it was all game for Burke. Then he would go on to seemingly unconnected events and inventions down through the ages until ... he wows you with a connection, a conclusion, you never saw coming.

Case in point, this show from somewhere around 1984. It was called "Eat, Drink and Be Merry. It began with plastic, then talked about credit cards, the concept of credit, which leads back to the Dukes of Burgundy back about the time Joan of Arc was running around.

The Dukes used credit to buy better armor for their army. This forced their enemy, the Swiss, to invent a new military  formation to hold Burgundy off. That formation employed pikemen formed in a square. To be a pikeman in a pike square required about zero skill. No skill equaled bigger armies. Muskets replaced pikes, muskets weren't very accurate so the same armies kept the same square like formation.

By the French Revolution, armies were getting enormous. Napoleon needed quite a few men, he recognized that an army was as good as what it was eating, so, the French invented bottled food. Which quickly became canned food for armies and navies. Canned food, however, would occasionally spoil.

In the mid-Nineteenth Century people blamed bad air for the spoilage. The race to discover the source of bad air led to the invention of air conditioning and refrigeration. Sir James Dewar went off in a slightly different tangent and invented the thermos. The thermos was adapted for use to hold liquid hydrogen and oxygen.

Liquid oxygen and hydrogen fueled rocket propulsion and, viola, you have the Saturn V rocket and men landing on the moon

Simple, right?

Here's the thing that gets me about all this, until the very end, no one involved in this incredible chain of events and inventions and innovations had the slightest clue where it was all going to end up.

Everybody in this chain acted, invented, innovated, created, for their own reasons, to their own ends. The Burgundy dukes had no conception of air conditioning, never mind liquid oxygen. Yet without them Neil Armstrong never takes a stroll on the moon.

So, wow and what does this have to do with family law?

Just this – when you are involved in a divorce – amicable, contested, mediated, arbitrated, flat-out courtroom contest – and you say or act in the heat of a moment or moments, you have about as much say over the resulting consequences of those words and/or actions as any of the people in James Burke's long, long lines of connections.

The only definite is that it will, somehow, someplace, come back to you. And not in a positive, "one small step for man" way.

10. Attorneys

We've established by now that I am, indeed an attorney. I have an office of more lawyers. I interact with many more lawyers in court, in conferences, in mediation, in depositions, in line at the local coffee shop, in the lawyer business group I belong to, at Bar functions and so on.

So, I have a few opinions about lawyers.

Here goes.

§

Over the last few years, as Bill James' sabermetrics followers have had increasing influence across Major League Baseball, virtually running teams like the Arizona Diamondbacks, Astros, and Dodgers, a new measure of player value has emerged.

Wins Above Replacement. W.A.R. The math behind WAR is daunting and is constantly changing. It incorporates every conceivable baseball stat available and then some – for the last couple of years, the new brand of stat gurus have even incorporated where balls in play land (witness the fact that the Dodgers were recently banned from using laser pointers in Citifield *during* games against the Mets.)

It doesn't help that the formula for WAR is constantly changing. If you don't pay attention and took a casual look at BaseballReference.com every once in a while you might think that Babe Ruth, the all-time WAR leader in baseball history (remember, he was the best left-handed pitcher in the American League before he was, well, Babe Ruth), had somehow lost effectiveness over the last couple of years.

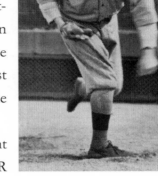

Despite its inherent complexity and opaqueness, WAR is grounded in a pretty great concept – the value of a player compared to an 'average' player at the same position. Or, to sort of quote the stats guys, 'how much better is a major leaguer than the guy who would replace him on the roster if he got hurt or retired?' It's measured in games, as in 'how many more wins did Babe Ruth account for over an average player'.

In Ruth's case, it's enormous. In 1923, for instance, Ruth accounted for 14 wins. In a 154-game season, that's incredible – the Yankees won 98 games that year, according to WAR they would have been an 84-win team without him and not the World Series Champs.

It's all a little confusing until you get used to the idea of what WAR represents. Being better than the average. The regular. The guy holding the spot until a star comes along. The proverbial journeyman player.

So, why am I writing about this in what is ostensibly a law memoir?

Like Major League Baseball, law is a field where, once you get in via law school and the Bar exam, everyone is assumed to be competent. You can be as ticked off as you want when your favorite team loses a game in the bottom of the tenth because a utility infielder drops a pop-up, but you have to admit, no matter what, that he's one of the top 750 baseball players in the world. At least that night.

Everyone who graduates law school and survives the Bar exam to get licensed to practice is presumed, like MLB players, to be competent. Unlike MLB players and members of other professions, like doctors, attorneys can practice in any area they want at any time.

A lawyer, in theory, can do a closing at 9:30, draft a will at 10:45, attend a court hearing for a divorce case at noon, interview an accident victim at 1:30 ... well, you get the picture.

That lawyer is the baseline that AWAR (Attorney Wins Against Replacement) should be measured. That lawyer has a WAR of 0.0. (By the way, WAR can be negative, meaning someone actually cost his team wins, so ...).

So, about my WAR. I work solely in family law. That's it. I've been doing it for a while and I'm good at it. I know the judges, the mediators, the other attorneys. I've seen and handled almost every conceivable scenario within this realm. If an attorney dabbling in family law, is a 0.0, I believe I'm at least a 4.42. I mean, there are no Babe Ruths anymore.

Where's a 4.42 WAR/year put me? Well, dead center in the top 100 WAR players in MLB history is one of my favorite players of all time, Chipper Jones at 85.0 – he accounted for 85 wins over his career. His position there is pretty  safe – no currently active player over 30 has any kind of chance of reaching him.

He's there because he was rock steady over his career. He played two positions well (defense helps immensely in WAR) and was startlingly consistent, even through injury. and, he could handle pressure – ask any Mets fan. He averaged about 4.42 WAR per season.

That's what you should be looking for in an attorney.

§

Here's a story a friend of mine in New England relayed to me.

I decided to get some writing done at Starbucks one recent late afternoon. It just seemed like a preferable alternative – coffee, headphones, no chance of being interrupted. I had been there a couple of blissful hours (way too much coffee, though) when around 5:20 a tall guy around 50, wearing a dress shirt and tie, no jacket, shirt sleeves rolled up, plopped down a couple of seats away, there was no one else near us.

He sat, no coffee, put a thin file folder on the table, began to scroll through his iPhone, every sign of waiting for someone. That somebody showed up at exactly 5:30, (I looked). It was a guy, short, lean, with a perpetual scowl and the air of a problem child. (I know the type). He was in jeans and polo shirt. They obviously know each other, say their 'hellos', sort of shake hands, a few words are exchanged, they toss their keys on the table, and head out to the parking lot . . .

Polo guy comes back with a loose-leaf notebook about 2 feet thick with hundreds of tabs. Drops it on table and whole place shakes with the echo. Tie guy comes back with a look of resignation.

I know at once tie guy is a lawyer, polo guy is his client. They go get coffee, come back, sit and start talking. Loudly. They are 5 feet away and I can hear them over Nick Cave and the Bad

Seeds ... so I turn Nick off and listen ... because why not, they're intruding on the entire coffee shop, obviously not all that concerned with privacy issues.

Tie guy is indeed a lawyer, polo guy is a free-lance orthopedic surgeon being sued for malpractice by a guy who claims that his knee is screwed up forever. As someone with a rebuilt ACL, I am now totally caught up in it. Plus, they're getting louder. Doc interrupts Lawyer's every 10th word or so with the kind of legalese only someone who has learned all their law from years of *Law & Order* repeats employs.

It doesn't take long before Doc starts ripping through his notebook, tearing at the tabs, hands flying all over the place, arguing points of law with all the finesse a doctor pretending to be an attorney can. He begins laying out his case, the one he has obviously been working on since he found out he needed an attorney. He's getting loud, the baristas are noticing, everyone on my side of the store moves to the other.

Doc is halfway through a soliloquy of things Lawyer is missing when Lawyer stands. He picks up the thin file folder, removes one thin page. "I'm getting a refill," he announces to the room and picks up his cup, "while I'm gone, read this," he drops the sheet on the table, "it's from the last depo, it's the nurse's – your nurse – just read it ...Want anything?"

Doc shakes his head, Lawyer heads for the counter, shadow of a smile playing across his face. Doc reads the page, his face turns white, he starts frantically flipping through the loose-leaf notebook. I'm immediately reminded of Professor Kingsford in *The Paper Chase*, "You won't find the answer in the casebook, Mr. Brooks."

Lawyer hung around the counter, when the barista asked him what he wanted he said, "A beer" before he handed her his cup. As she was doing the refill, Doc was packing up, thirty-pound notebook under his arm, he waved a weak goodbye to

Lawyer and headed out. He left the thin file folder on the table.

That's when it hit me that lawyer guy invited that guy to Starbucks because that was the best place to give him bad news and keep him somewhat under control. Right from the Jerry Maguire playbook. Except done a lot better.

§

There are basically two ways an attorney can approach a divorce. One is to listen to the client carefully for ten minutes, cut them off, and tell them how 'they' are going to proceed based on how *the attorney* thinks it should go. Because they're the expert, the field is complicated, the client is too emotionally invested to make decisions, and … well, you get the picture.

This approach usually involves months of promises, shallow follow-through, continuances, and a deep immersion into a process that is hardly a paragon of efficiency.

Movies are made about this approach. One of the best is the Coen Brothers' *Intolerable Cruelty*. In this case, the title says it all. Fun movie, no one would ever want to partake of even a sliver of it in real life.

They don't make movies about the other approach – the logic-based, rational method. Good drama (and comedies, for that matter) needs tension and conflict. The first approach has that. The second, my approach, does not. It would be boring if it wasn't your divorce we were working on.

My approach relies on a lot more than a few minutes listening. It requires interaction, communication, and problem solving on the fly. It requires a solid combination of common sense and book sense. It requires my filling you in on what you need to know; it occasionally requires me to tell you things you may not necessarily want to hear.

It does not involve getting mired down in the system, it most certainly does not involve endless promises and no follow through. It does involve research, analysis, communication, figuring out what is best for you and your family and working toward that goal quickly and efficiently.

§

Written with my great friends at Freed Marcroft LLC in Hartford, Connecticut.

We've been thinking a lot about communications lately. Which is a good thing. The only lawyers who don't need to study communication are the ones who never talk with clients. There are some out there; they certainly aren't us.

We were recently reminded of a famous, influential, comedy team out of the '60's – Bob and Ray. Bob and Ray's entire act was based on communication, or lack thereof.

Flipping through some of the old clips from thirty years of late-night TV appearances – they were steady guests from Johnny Carson to David Letterman – one thing really hit us: Bob and Ray should be required viewing in every law school in the country and every state's Bar association's continuing ed classes.

Two examples stand out.

The first, their iconic *STOA* skit. There are many variations on the bit; the basics are this: Bob is interviewing the president of the Slow Talkers of America. The results are what you'd expect: Bob asks a question, and Ray takes his sweet time answering.

"Tell me, what does STOA stand for?"

"The .... Slow .... Talkers .... of .... America."

It goes on, always with the same pace. After a [short] while Bob can't take it anymore and begins to fill in what he's sure is where the answer's going.

"Where is the STOA based out of?"

"We .... are .... located .... in ....Glen .... Falls .... New ...."

"York, right, it's New York."

"Hampshire."

And so it goes. Bob is increasingly frustrated, is almost always wrong, gets more frustrated, becomes fidgety, belligerent, learns nothing.

Perfect.

We're family law attorneys. We need to hear everything about our clients. At the same time, we need to understand it's really, really hard to tell anyone, never mind an almost stranger, details of your family life.

We can't force it, and we definitely can't anticipate answers — even to the simple questions. We have to let the slow talker, fast talker (FTOA, it's in the skit, too), close talker, and everyone else take whatever time they need to tell us what we need to know.

The second bit, we think, really speaks to the law profession: *Whooping Crane Facts*. This time Bob is interviewing a world renown expert on the whooping crane. Bob has a script, and Ray is a whooping crane enthusiast who isn't bound by answering a specific question. He's the kind of person who takes any question as an invitation to gush facts. He stomps all over Bob's list of carefully thought out questions.

Which Bob sticks to . . . no matter what. As the bit goes on, Bob continues to ask questions that have already been answered . . . which leads to even more breathless information that now just overwhelms Bob . . . which makes him ask more already answered questions . . . while he screws up everything he's already been told. Apparently, concentrating on a list of questions isn't all that conducive to active listening.

It's an intricate, beautifully choreographed, all verbal skit that is funny every time you hear it.

On TV or YouTube.

It is emphatically not at all funny to experience. As a client.

Interviewing a client isn't taught in most law schools; there are no classes in how to listen. Though there should be.

Our clients are unique. The way they talk, how they talk, why they talk, and what they choose to talk about are equally unique. There's no script of questions, just like there's no set way we're going to approach a client's case.

Which, we're sure, is a good thing. Poor Bob probably would have had much more fun listening to Ray if he hadn't been so intent on hearing what he wanted to hear.

I added this after we published this as a joint blog piece:

Recently met with a gentleman. We spent about an hour and a half together. I asked maybe 5 questions and interjected a few "tell me more about that" and "hmmm's." At the end of our time together, he said, "I feel like you really get me and what's important to me." Mind you, I never offered advice or opinions and certainly not judgments. Instead, I kept him talking about his fears, his concerns and his goals. And I listened. When I wanted to ask a burning legal question, I listened. When I wanted to know more about something, I listened. When I wanted him to speed up, I listened. When I wanted him to slow down, I listened. When he was silent, I listened. Clients don't come to us for a lecture, for a Q&A session, or for an advisory opinion when we've done no case work-up; they come to us because they have a problem and because they want someone to listen.

§

This was written with my friend Jackie Bedard at *Carolina Family Estate Planning* in Cary, North Carolina.

There's a best seller out about Elizabeth Holmes and Theranos. If this doesn't ring a bell – Holmes was the twenty-something Steve Jobs dress-alike, Silicon Valley tech head who formed a company, Theranos, to use cutting edge technology to do full blood tests with only a drop of blood. Less invasive, faster, it would revolutionize the multi-billion-dollar lab services industry.

Holmes raised a ton of money, became the youngest billionaire in Silicon Valley's history. The sky was the limit. For her and Theranos.

Or, would have been had any of it been real. But, it wasn't. It was almost entirely fake. Smoke, mirrors, a great PR firm, a fawning financial press, photogenic/charismatic CEO, great idea perfectly marketed, an all-star Board of Directors, and great market timing made it seem real for far too long until a Wall Street Journal reporter, John Carryrou began to sniff around. And, boy, did it reek.

The technology was never there, never close. Tests were either conducted using standard industry machines, or faked, the few done by Theranos' machines were so inaccurate as to be worthless.

Tech guys, sales people, execs, a few other employees had questions for years as they watched the company promise investors and customers things they could not provide. Bringing a concern over that to Holmes or her COO or any number of executives usually led to immediate termination and a perp walk by security out of the building.

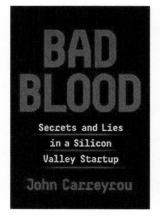

Over the years, dozens of employees – from janitors to tech wizards to engineers and salespeople – quit or were fired over their concerns about Theranos' business practices and representations. All these ex-employees knew the truth of what was really going on with Theranos. Yet, not one word of the growing fraud leaked.

The reason was simple: Theranos tossed a long, nasty, complete non-disclosure agreement at every new employee. No signature, no job. Terminated employees were hounded, sometimes for years, by letters – if not visits – from lawyers 'just to remind them of their duty to the company.'

Holmes spent a fortune on a top-flight law firm renown for acting more like the Sopranos than Ally McBeal. She hired one of their partners as her General Counsel. Between the general counsel and the law firm the non-disclosures were enforced with all the subtlety of KGB Gulag trials.

It was brutal, they sued and threatened with impunity.

No one got a warning letter, they got a 'do this or die' manifesto of legal and extralegal threats . . . those who didn't get surprise, drop-in visits from a Theranos lawyer or 'investigator.'

In all the recitation of lawyer bullying in *Bad Blood* – and there's a dizzying amount – the one constant is this: everyone caved, usually upon first contact with the lawyers.

The pattern was clear: sign non-disclosure, get hired, grow concerned over fraud/lying/scam, voice concerns, be fired and escorted out of building, letter or visit or both about not violating the non-disclosure/ never speak of it again until reporter from Wall Street Journal comes along and federal indictments are on the way down.

In all this depressingly consistent narrative, a few employees consulted their own lawyers. Every discussion but one in the book went pretty much like this:

"Hey, I signed a ten-page non-disclosure, but – "

"Ten pages?"

"Yeah, but – "

"Must be thorough, I wouldn't mess with it."

The exception went to an attorney, gave him all her documents, filled him in on the extent of the fraud and the harassment activities of Theranos and was told, "That's awful, but the law firm that did this is an awful big hitter, best not to mess with them."

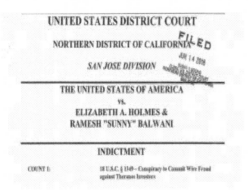

So, here's the thing with all this, and the reason we – a family law firm and an estate planning firm – are writing about this: no one in this fascinating though appalling book consulted with an attorney who exclusively practiced in employment law.

Every ex-employee went to their parent's lawyer, the guy that did their closing, the woman who did their mother's will, the firm that grandma used when she slipped and fell in Stop & Shop, and, worse, the brother-in-law who just graduated law school.

In short, attorneys who would take one look at a dauntingly long, small-print, 'airtight' agreement drafted by a leading law firm and immediately discount everything else, the fraud, the business practices, the harassments, and fold.

About the fraud, by the way: Holmes raised $700 million from thousands of investors based on lies; made promises she had no hope of keeping to Walgreens and a dozen other companies; botched thousands of blood tests with ongoing repercussions for patients that still haven't been resolved; and more.

The odds are pretty high that had anyone gone to an employment law attorney with their stories, that lawyer would have leaned backed, sighed, and filled them in on the California whistleblower statutes, and a whole lot more.

No one in the 352 pages of *Bad Blood* consulted the kind of attorney who would actually know the law by virtue of concentrating their practice in it over years. The only people in the book who talked to the right lawyers were Elizabeth Holmes and John Carryrou – who had access to the Wall Street Journal's attorneys.

Bad Blood is the perfect illustration of why it is so – so – important to engage attorneys who concentrate in the area of the law that you happen to need help with.

11. Divorce

This is the age of instant gratification and entitlement, and even faster information and communication.

That's the primary reason I see the divorce rate increasing in the next decade. I talk to people about divorce all day every day. One thing that hits me often is the feeling that some couples are throwing in the towel too soon and too easily. Of course, in cases of abuse (physical, substance, and/or emotional), getting divorced is often the better choice than staying together. As it is for anyone in a toxic relationship.

For everyone else, though, it sometimes feels as if it's just more expedient than working out a problem(s). So, before coming to a divorce lawyer, try one or more of the following:

- Listen to listen. Don't listen to react. Don't listen to reply. Don't listen to defend. Listen to listen. Then listen some more. Way back in the olden days of the 1980's some genius in the Committee to Re-Elect the President decided that Bruce Springsteen's Born in the USA was a terrific song to play as good ol' Ronald Reagan took the stage for a speech. He, obviously, never got past the title, because I'm pretty sure "Born down in a dead man's town, the first kick I got was when I hit the ground," wasn't exactly a message Ronnie could get behind. So, listen.

- There're a million love songs out there about 'love is the drug' and how it 'conquers all' and overcomes adversity and all that. Those songs are catchy and lovely and were probably pretty big hits and are utterly wrong. Money "makes the world go around, the world go around" and life is "all about the Benjamins." For the simple reason that the stress of money issues is probably the number one killer of marriages. Get on the same page about money. Have a budget and stick to it. Plan to save and actually save. Develop an emergency fund. Financial stress pours over into every facet of marriage.

- Do things together. Do things apart. You married your best friend. I believe your spouse should remain your best friend, but I also believe that a healthy marriage needs a balance of togetherness time and time invested in yourself and outside interests.

• Express your feelings but chose your words carefully. Don't create a soundbite. Soundbites are remembered forever regardless of what the underlying message was. And by forever, I mean FOREVER. Think of this: how many movies or TV series have you suffered through after having realized ten, twenty minutes in that the entire thing could be solved, resolved, wrapped up, ended if the two main protagonists expressed their feelings? Oh, and by the way, how many of those shows jumped the shark when those feelings were finally revealed in, like, season six? Cheers, anyone?

• Be accountable. Blaming the other is non-productive. It is a rare case that one person is causing all the problems.

• Compromise. A little accommodation can go a long way.

• Don't sweat the small stuff. As the book says, "It really is small stuff."

• Keep lust alive. Remember when you first started dating or when your relationship became sexual. Don't fall into the roommate trap. Keep lust alive.

• Do random acts of kindness. That might be an unexpected flirty text, performing a chore without being asked or plan a surprise date night.

• Be happy with who you are. No one else is responsible for your happiness, and if you aren't happy with yourself, you are very unlikely to be happy in a relationship with anyone else.

§

...I have seen the beauty of good, and the ugliness of evil, and have recognized that the wrongdoer has a nature related to my own — not of the same blood or birth, but of the same mind, and possessing a share of the divine.

And so, none of them can hurt me.

No one can implicate me in ugliness.

Nor can I feel angry at my relative, or hate him.

We were born to work together like feet, hands, and eyes, like the two rows of teeth, upper and lower.

To obstruct each other is unnatural.

To feel anger at someone, to turn your back on him: these are obstructions. ~ Marcus Aurelius

§

I love puzzles. I hate being bored. That means, of course, that I hate working on the same puzzle all over again – because, then, it's not a puzzle. It's a routine.

That, I think, is at the heart of my choosing to work in family law. You see, every divorce is unique.

When people, family, and emotions are involved nothing is routine, no set of facts ever repeats. Going from one case to the next doesn't mean just resetting the board, most of the time the board has changed as well.

Again, no truer words have ever been written than Tolstoy's, "All happy families are alike; every unhappy family is unhappy in its own way."

Another thing – I abhor … unfairness. Unfairness is rife in divorce law. Everyone going through a divorce is vulnerable in one way or another.

Many are in position to be used and/or allow themselves to be used. I see people taken advantage of every day; exploited by lawyers who don't understand the nuances of divorce law; oppressed by an overloaded court system; still bending to the will of a controlling spouse.

Lastly, unlike a lot of professionals and a lot of lawyers in a lot of fields, I get to experience tangible outcomes with my clients. I see them through an unhappy, stressful time in their lives and am there to see them start over. That is amazingly gratifying.

And, when I go along the journey with them, I inevitably learn more about myself.

Acknowledgements

Mike Schilawski – for taking a chance on me as a baby lawyer and encouraging me to think holistically and strategically about our client's futures and for continuing to be a listening ear

Sally Sharp – a Kentucky gal who got through to this Tennessee girl about how being a family lawyer was the shit (and gave me a top-notch reference to Schilawski)

My grandmothers – one who taught me enjoying the finer things in life, like Diet Coke, Snickers and Iced Tea, while watching soap operas and playing Monopoly and checkers, but also would conveniently forget her glasses at the store or library and taught me math and reading, while boosting my self-esteem at an early age AND the other who taught me the value of hard work and overcoming adversity (and an enjoyment of vodka and scotch, which soothed both of those points)

My grandfather – who taught me to be accountable, responsible and how to fix damn near everything mechanical

My parents – who were mere children when they had a child, took me to both of their high school graduations and pushed me hard to have different experiences than they did

Numerous high school teachers and college professors – who encouraged me to challenge my beliefs and expand my exposure to new and different ideas

My friends and coaches within HTM – for jumpstarting my personal and spiritual journey

Roland – for encouraging me to be me and helping me rediscover my voice

The Warren family – we may not be biologically related but you all are my family. Thank you for your endless support, understanding and kind words over the years. And for reminding me that I don't have to be anyone but me.

And to Mitzi and Alex – words cannot adequately express the gratefulness I have for each of you and the lessons I have learned and continue to learn about trust, love and authenticity from the both of you

About the Author

Jenny Bradley is a jock, a nerd, and a lawyer. None of that is mutually exclusive.

She devotes her practice to working with clients in family law matters. But you know that now, assuming you read the book in front of this and didn't just skip to the 'About the Author' page.

What Jenny doesn't mention in the pages before this is that her experience and successes in family law have been recognized publicly. *Business North Carolina Magazine* has named her to their Legal Elite Award List in 2009, 2010, 2011, 2012, 2014, 2015, and 2016 an honor especially notable as it is an award chosen by fellow North Carolina attorneys.

She was named as a Rising Star by North Carolina's Super Lawyer publication in 2011, 2012 and 2013. She aged out of that category not too long ago and has been namd a Super Lawyer in 2015, 2016, 2017 and 2018.

That's the lawyer stuff.

When not in the office, or a court house, you'll find Jenny in all kinds of places, like the softball diamond, the local bookstore, on a bicycle, enjoying a great meal with fine wine . . . or beer . . . or bourbon, attending professional develeopment seminars, traveling, and, yes, still kicking butt in 80's trivia contests.

JENNY BRADLEY

49954803R00114

Made in the USA
Columbia, SC
01 February 2019